HOW I LEARNED TO TRADE LIKE TOM SOSNOFF AND TONY BATTISTA

BOOK ONE: TRADE MECHANICS

By Tony Rihan

ISBN: 0615857752
ISBN-13: 9780615857756

Library of Congress Control Number: 2013914511
Antonio Rihan, La Jolla, California

DEDICATION

To my beloved parents, Gladys and Eduardo. From you I learned the true value of hard work, controlling expenses and most importantly, putting family first. You guys gave me the foundation that allowed me to be successful in life. I also want to thank my wife Chris, the most beautiful and intelligent person in the world. You have always supported me and believed in me, allowing me to create my own path in this world. Everything that I possess or have achieved in life I owe to you guys. I love you & I miss you!

ACKNOWLEDGMENTS

I want to thank the two most generous people that I have ever met; Mr. Tom Sosnoff and Mr. Tony Battista. They not only are the two best traders in the world, but also the kindest and most giving. They share all their knowledge and experience without holding anything back. Normally, experts in their fields are very reluctant to share and teach what they know, but not these two fine gentlemen.

I would also like to thank Consuelo my assistant for helping me write this book, and Omar my wonderful graphic designer who helped with all the images.

CONTENTS

INTRODUCTION

I was raised in an entrepreneurial family. My Dad grew up in a family that did ok financially, and my grandparents had enough money to pay for my Dad's education, but not enough to help out my Dad jump start his financial future.

I had always been a straight A student in High School, through college and also during my MBA. Normally good grades don't mean much, but what they did for me was to give me confidence, as I believed I was smart enough to be successful in life in any field that I chose.

My five favorite things in life are starting new companies, trading, my family, golf and eating. So at my Dad's suggestion, I started companies in the fields or industries that I loved the most (Golf, Pens and Financial Instruments)

In 2007, I started a small Hedge fund. I had traded stocks for more than 20 years since I was about 17 years old, with good results, and I thought that since I was good at math and finance, I could run a hedge fund. Boy, was I wrong.

By 2008, I had lost 35% of the funds value. I became depressed, as I'd rarely failed in any business venture that I had tried before. After seeing me like this, My Dad asked me what was wrong. I told him what had happened with the fund, and about all the money I'd lost. He told me that I needed to further my education in trading if I wanted to do this type of venture professionally, and also this could prevent such a loss from happening again.

Since I was interested in trading derivatives, we needed to find someone that could help me in that field. By coincidence, our family lawyers were from Chicago, the Mecca for options trading, and so we asked them to recommend the Top Trader in the country, in the hope that I could learn from him.

After they did some investigating, the name Tom Sosnoff came from a friend of one of the firm's lawyers with experience in that field. The guy said Tom was the best, and best of all, that he also liked teaching.

After further investigating, I found that one way to gain access to Tom's insight would be through a company called Investools, that offered investor education. Tom was involved in this company through the trading firm he had created, Think or Swim (TOS).

I proceeded to take all the online and live classes that Tom taught. In one of those classes I met Mr. Tony Battista, and the other Investools and TOS teachers/traders that gave me my foundation as a trader.

From that day on, I have been following both "My Sensei's", TOM & TONY!!

THE GOAL OF BOOK ONE

Our goal is to teach you the fundamental trade mechanics and rules of high probability trading. You will learn that trading must be mechanical, and that successful trading has some very specific rules that must be followed if you are to avoid losses, and gain the highest probability of profit.

In the second book, I will show you insights into how Tom and Tony trade. That book will help you further refine and perfect your skills as a trader.

The only way to learn how to trade is by actually trading. For example, you cannot learn how to play golf by reading a book or watching a video; you need to go out and hit some balls and "play golf". It's the same with trading; you learn by doing - by trading. Trading well is not a function of time to me; it is a function of the number of trades:

- Below 10,000 trades, you will be a rookie.
- For every additional 10,000 trades that you do, you will improve exponentially.
- Every trader is different of course, but I became a consistently profitable trader after I did about 20,000 trades.

Let's get started, and Good Luck Trading!

THE PRODUCTS WE TRADE

Tom always likes to say that we need to know how to use all the "clubs" in our golf bag. It is important to know at least the basics of each instrument, and how they related to each other in the market.

Here are the basic definitions.

STOCK

A **stock** is a type of security that signifies ownership in a corporation and represents a claim on part of the corporation's assets and earnings.

There are two main types of stock: common and preferred.
- **Common stock** usually entitles the owner to vote at shareholders' meetings and to receive dividends.
- **Preferred stock** generally does not have voting rights, but has a higher claim on assets and earnings than the common shares. For example, owners of preferred stock receive dividends before common shareholders, and they also have priority, in the event that a company goes bankrupt and is liquidated.

A holder of stock (a stockholder, or shareholder) has a claim to a part of the corporation's assets and earnings. In other words, a shareholder is an owner of the company. Ownership is determined by the number of shares a person owns relative to the number of outstanding shares. For example, if a company has 1,000 shares of stock outstanding and one person owns 100 shares, that person would own and have claim to 10% of the company's assets.

OPTIONS

Options are contracts giving the owner the right to buy or sell a financial asset at a fixed price (called the "strike price") for a specific period of time. That period of time could be as short as a day or as long as a couple of years, depending on the option. The seller of the option contract has the obligation to conduct the trade, if and when the owner exercises the right to buy or sell the asset.

The Two Types of Options: Calls & Puts

- **Call Options**

   When you buy a call, it gives you the right (but not the obligation) to buy a specific stock at a specific price per share within a specific time frame. A good way to remember this is to think that you have the right to "call" the stock away from somebody.

   If you sell a call, you have the obligation to sell the stock at a specific price per share within a specific time frame, if the call buyer decides to invoke the right to buy the stock at that price.

- **Put Options**

   When you buy a put, it gives you the right (but not the obligation) to sell a specific stock at a specific price per share within a specific time frame. A good way to remember this is that you have the right to "put" stock to somebody.

   If you sell a put, you have the obligation to buy the stock at a specific price per share within a specific time frame if the put buyer decides to invoke the right to sell the stock at that price.

Combinations of Calls & Puts Create The Strategies

Every strategy that you will learn is based on those two products. You can buy or sell calls, and you can buy or sell puts. Also, you can buy or sell them at different prices and on different expiration periods.

Complex strategies combine call and puts, and may also include stock positions on the same stock. Don't worry, complex does not mean hard to understand. It is my job to help you understand each and every one of these strategies, so you can play with a full set of clubs.

FUTURES

A **future** is a financial contract obligating the buyer to purchase an asset (or the seller to sell an asset) at a predetermined future date and price. The asset can be for example a physical commodity or a financial instrument. Futures contracts detail the quality and quantity of the underlying asset, and they are standardized to facilitate trading on a futures exchange. Some futures contracts may call for physical delivery of the asset, while others are settled in cash. The futures markets are characterized by the ability to use very high leverage relative to stock markets.

Futures can be used either to hedge, or to speculate on the price movement of the underlying asset. For example, a producer of gold could use futures to hedge, and lock in a certain price and thus reduce his risk. On the other hand, anybody could speculate on the price movement of gold, by going long or short using futures.

The primary difference between options and futures is that options give the holder the *right* to buy or sell the underlying asset at expiration, while the holder of a futures contract is *obligated* to fulfill the terms of his/her contract.

FOREX - ALSO KNOWN AS FX

The **Forex** market is where currencies are traded. It is the largest, most liquid market in the world, with an average traded value that exceeds $1.9 trillion per day and includes all the currencies in the world. The Forex market is open 24 hours a day, five days a week and currencies are traded worldwide among the major financial centers of London, New York, Tokyo, Zürich, Frankfurt, Hong Kong, Singapore, Paris and Sydney.

There is no central marketplace for currency exchange; trade is conducted "over the counter" (OTC).

AN INDEX
In the case of financial markets, an index is an imaginary portfolio of securities, representing a particular market or a portion of it. Each index has its own calculation methodology, and is usually expressed in terms of a change from a base value. Thus, the percentage change is more important than the actual numeric value.

- **Stock and bond market indices** are used to construct index mutual funds and exchange-traded funds (ETFs), whose portfolios mirror the components of the index.
- **The SPX (S&P 500) index** is the most closely followed; it is the granddaddy of them all. The Dow Jones Industrial average (Dow 30) used to occupy this space, but several years ago it lost the # 1 spot to the SPX, because its size more truly represents what is going on in the market overall.
- Other closely watched indices are the NDX (Nasdaq 100), and the RUT (Russell 2000), representing both the technology sector and the small cap stocks respectably.

EXCHANGE-TRADED FUND - ETF
An ETF is a security that tracks an index, commodity or basket of assets like an index fund, but trades like a stock on an exchange. Technically, you can't actually invest in an index, so index mutual funds and exchange-traded funds (based on indices) allow investors to invest in securities representing broad market segments and/or the total market.

Because it trades like a stock, an ETF does not have its net asset value (NAV) calculated every day, like a mutual fund does.

By owning an ETF, you have the diversification of an index fund as well as the ability to sell short, buy on margin and purchase as little as one share. Another advantage is that the expense ratios for most ETFs are lower than those of the average mutual fund. When buying and selling ETFs, you have to pay the same commission to your broker that you'd pay on any regular order.

One of the most widely known ETFs is called the Spider (SPDR), which tracks the S&P 500 index, and trades under the symbol SPY.

Other widely own ETFs are QQQ (representing the Nasdaq), the IWM, (representing the Russell 2000), the XLF (representing the financial sector) and the XLK (representing the technology sector).

Here is a list of some of the most liquid and more popular ETFs that you can trade:

INDEX ETFs
- SPY   S&P 500 INDEX
- DIA   DOW 30 INDEX
- MDY   MID CAP INDEX
- QQQQ   NASDAQ 100 INDEX
- IWM   Russell 2000 Index

BEARISH ETFs
- SDS   DOUBLE SHORT S&P 500 INDEX
- QID   DOUBLE SHORT NASDAQ INDEX
- FAZ   TRIPLE SHORT RUSSEL 2000

BOND ETFs
- SHY   iShares Lehman 1-3 Year
- IEF   iShares Lehman 7-10 Year
- TLT   iShares Lehman 20+ Year
- LQD   iShares Investment Grade Bonds
- HYG   iShares High Yield Grade Bonds
- JNK   Barclays High Yield Rated B Corporate Bonds
- TBT   Ultra Short 20 year Treasury

SECTOR ETFs
- BBH   Biotech HOLDRs Trust
- IYR   I shares US Real Estate
- OIH   Oil Services HOLDRs Trust
- PPH   Pharmaceutical HOLDRs Trust

- RTH   ML Retail Holders
- SMH   ML Semiconductor SPDR
- XHB   SPDR Homebuilders
- XLE   Energy Sector SPDR
- XLF   Financial Select Sector SPDR
- XLI   Industrial Select Sector SPDR
- XLK   Technology Sector SPDR
- XLP   Consumer Staples SPDR
- XLU   Utilities EFT
- XLV   Heath Care SPDR

COUNTRY AND INTERNATIONAL ETFs
- EEM   EMERGING MARKET INDEX
- EWW   iShares MSCI Mexico index
- FXI   iShares MSCI China 25 index
- EWG   iShares MSCI Germany
- EWI   iShares MSCI Italy
- EWJ   iShares MSCI Japan
- EWZ   iShares MSCI Brazil
- EWA   iShares MSCI Australia

COMMODITY ETFs
- GLD   Street TRACKS Gold Trust
- SLV   iShares Silver Trust
- USO   U.S. Oil Fund
- XLB   Materials Select Sector SPDR
- XLE   Energy Sector SPDR
- USG   U.S. Natural Gas
- DBA   Power Shares DB Agriculture
- PHO   Power Shares Water Resources

CURRENCY ETFs
- UUP   Power Shares DB US Dollar Index Bullish
- FXE   Rydex Euro Currency Shares

- FXA   Currency Shares Australian Dollar Trust
- FXB   Currency Shares British Pound Sterling Trust
- FXC   Currency Shares Canadian Dollar Trust
- FXM   Currency Shares Mexican Peso Trust
- FXS   Currency Shares Swedish Krona Trust
- FXF   Currency Shares Swiss Franc Trust

Don't worry if some of these meanings aren't crystal clear at first. That's normal. Just keep forging ahead, and everything will become more apparent over time.

BASIC TRADING CONCEPTS

If you want to become a "great trader", a complete understanding of these terms is very important.

LONG
When you're talking about options and stocks, "long" implies a position of ownership. After you have purchased an option or a stock, you are considered to be long that security in your account. If you are long a stock or an option, you will benefit if the price of the underlying goes up.

SHORT
If you've sold an option or a stock without actually owning it, you are then considered to be "short" that security in your account. That's actually one of the interesting things about options - you can sell something that you don't actually own, but when you do, you may be obligated to do something at a later date. If you are short a stock or an option, you will benefit if the price of the underlying goes down.

STRIKE PRICE
The strike price is a pre-agreed price per share at which stock may be bought or sold under the terms of an option contract. Some people refer to the strike price as the "exercise price".

IN-THE-MONEY (ITM)

- **For call options**, this means the stock price is above the strike price. So if a call has a strike price of $20 and the stock is trading at $25, that option is said to be in-the-money.
- **For put options**, it means the stock price is below the strike price. So if a put has a strike price of $ 20 and the stock is trading at $ 15, that option is in-the-money.

OUT-OF-THE-MONEY (OTM)

- **For call options**, this means the stock price is below the strike price.
- **For put options**, this means the stock price is above the strike price. The cost of out-of-the-money (OTM) options consists entirely of "time value", also known as extrinsic value.

AT-THE-MONEY (ATM)

An option is "at-the-money" or ATM when the stock price is equal to the strike price. Since the two values are rarely exactly equal, when purchasing options the strike price closest to the stock price is typically called the "ATM strike."

For the rest of the book we will use the abbreviations ITM, OTM and ATM for in the money, out of the money and at the money options.

INTRINSIC VALUE

The Intrinsic Value is the ITM portion of an option's price. For this reason, only ITM options have intrinsic value.

EXTRINSIC VALUE

Extrinsic Value is the difference between an option's market price and its intrinsic value. Extrinsic value of a stock option is the extra money you are paying above the intrinsic value, in order to own that option.

Extrinsic value has three main components:
- Time Decay - also known as Theta.
- Implied Volatility - also known as Vega.
- Rho - A measure of the expected change in the option's theoretical value for a 1 percent change in interest rates. This is based on current interest rate carrying costs.

TIME VALUE (THETA)
The part of an option price that is based on its time to expiration.

Option price – intrinsic value = time value

If an option has no intrinsic value (i.e., it's OTM) its entire worth is based on time value.

EXERCISE
This occurs when the owner of an option invokes the right embedded in the option contract. In layman's terms, it means the option owner buys or sells the underlying stock at the strike price, and requires the option seller to take the other side of the trade.

ASSIGNMENT
When an option owner exercises the option, an option seller (or "writer") is assigned, and they must make good on their obligation. That means they are required to buy or sell the underlying stock at the strike price. Normally the assigned party is not happy, because it requires additional capital and resources, and they can also be assigned both long and short. In the short assignment it may mean that depending on the assigned date they may owe the dividend paid by that specific stock. So be careful about assignments!!

STOP-LOSS ORDERS
A stop order is an order to sell a stock or option when it reaches a certain price (the stop price). The order is designed to help limit an

investor's exposure to the markets on an existing position, and both Tom and Tony hate stop orders, by the way!

Here's how a stop-loss order works:
1. You select a stop price, usually below the current market price for an existing long position. By choosing a price below the current market, you're basically saying, "This is the lowest point where I would like to get out of my position".
2. When your position trades at or through your stop price, your stop order will be activated as a market order, seeking the best available market price at the time the order is triggered, in order to close out your position.

Stop orders don't provide much protection if the market is closed or trading is halted during the day. In those situations, stocks are likely to "gap" – and the next opening trade price after the trading halt may be significantly different from the price before the halt. If the stock gaps, your downside "protective" order will most likely trigger, but it's anybody's guess as to what the next available price will be.

Tom hates stop orders, because due to normal market volatility, they are almost always hit. The best way to avoid being stopped out is by trading small, and giving yourself enough duration to be right.

IMPLIED VOLATILITY
There are two types of volatility: historical and implied.

Historical Volatility
Historical volatility statistically measures a stock's price movement, based on its historical price performance. It is typically calculated by taking a standard deviation of the stock's daily closing price over a given period of time; e.g. one year, six months, three months and so on.

Implied Volatility

Implied volatility is derived from an option's current market price. Option prices do not imply a direction regarding the underlying stock's movement; they imply only probable distribution or expected price range of a stock. Increased implied volatility affects an option's expected time value, but not a stock's expected value.

In general, if a stock's price is flat, volatility should be low; if the stock's price is fluctuating, implied volatility should be high. The higher implied volatility is, the higher the resulting risk that the stock's price will move, which translates into demand from option sellers for higher premiums. In summary, the following factors can directly influence whether implied volatility will increase or decrease:

Factors that Increase Implied Volatility
- High demand (heavy option buying)
- Uncertainty in the underlying stock's price
- Pending events that may significantly impact the stock price such as:
  - o Earnings announcements
  - o Lawsuits
  - o Takeovers/mergers/acquisitions
  - o Economic announcements
  - o Business related news or announcements.

Factors that Decrease Implied Volatility
- Increasing supply (low demand/heavy option selling)
- Certainty in the underlying stock's price.

Implied volatility is a dynamic figure that changes based on activity in the options marketplace. When implied volatility increases, the price of options will usually increase as well, assuming all other things remain constant. So when implied volatility increases after a trade has been placed, it's good for the option owner and bad for the option seller.

Conversely, if implied volatility decreases after your trade is placed, the price of options usually decreases. That's good if you're an option seller and bad if you're an option owner.

VOLUME

Volume is defined as the number of shares or contracts traded during a given period of time in either a security or an entire market. It is simply the amount of shares that trade hands from sellers to buyers as a measure of activity. If a buyer of a stock purchases 100 shares from a seller, then the volume for that period increases by 100 shares, based on that transaction.

Volume and Open Interest are important, because you cannot trade something that is illiquid. You need stocks with at least 2,000,000 stocks a day traded. If the volume is lower, there are very few market makers, thus less liquidity. It has also has to be easy to borrow.

OPEN INTEREST

Open interest is the number of option contracts that exist for a particular stock. Obviously, if more of the volume on any given option is marked "to open" than "to close", open interest increases. Conversely, if more option trades are marked "to close" than "to open", interest decreases.

Open interest is a "logging number". In other words, it is not updated during the course of a trading day, but instead, it is officially posted by The OCC the morning after any given trading session, once the figures have been calculated. For the rest of the trading day the figure remains static.

If you see a very small number of open interest contracts, it can make it hard to get in and out of a position.

SLIPPAGE

Slippage is the edge you give away on your trades, by paying one or two or 3 pennies extra on your entry points. Your Slippage is the amount between the mid-price shown on your trading platform and the real price where you can get filled. Commissions are also considered slippage.

Mid-price ← slippage "→ real price

Slippage is also one of the differentiators between a very good trader, a professional trader, and a retail guy.

PROBABILITY OF EXPIRING AKA. PROBABILITY IN THE MONEY (ITM)

Probability of expiring is the likelihood that an option will expire at least $0.01 cents ITM at expiration. If you are short that option, then it is the probability that you have of keeping 100% of the premium received.

PROBABILITY OF TOUCHING

Probability of touching is the probability that your strike will be reached at any point during the trade. As a rule of thumb, the probability of touching is almost always 2x the probability of expiring. For example if an option has a 30% probability of expiring, it will probability have a 60% probability of touching.

STANDARD DEVIATION

In statistics and probability theory, standard deviation, represented by the symbol sigma (σ), shows how much variation or "dispersion" exists from the average (mean, or expected value).

In trading, we use one standard deviation to show us the expected range of an underlying to stay in a certain price range, and also for the probability of expiring within that range for about 68.27%. Furthermore, if we assume stocks have a simple normal price distribution, we can calculate what a one standard deviation move for the stock will be. On an annualized basis, the stock will stay within plus or minus one standard deviation roughly 68% of the time. This comes in handy when figuring out the potential range of movement for a particular stock.

Two standard deviations will give us a probability of 95.45% that an underlying will stay within that price range.

Three standard deviations will give us a probability of 99.73% that an underlying will stay within that price range.

In Summary, about 68.27% of the value or price range of a stock will lie within 1 standard deviation of the mean. Similarly, about 95.45% of the values or stock price range will lie within 2 standard deviations of the mean. Nearly all of the values (99.73%) lie within 3 standard deviations of the mean.

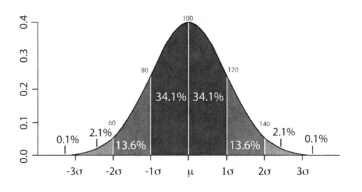

Black is less than one standard deviation from the mean. For the normal distribution, this accounts for 68.27% of the set; while two standard deviations from the mean (light grey, dark grey, and black on both sides) account for 95.45%, and three standard deviations (light grey, medium grey, and black) account for 99.73%.

OPTION GREEKS

The "Greeks" of calls and puts are calculated via mathematical models that rely on several variables, including:

- The stock's price
- The option's strike price
- The stock's estimated volatility
- The option's expiration date
- The current interest rate
- The dividends payable on the stock before the option expires.

Greeks are also dimensions of the risk involved in taking a position in an option (or other derivative). Each risk variable is a result of an imperfect assumption or relationship of the option with another underlying variable. Each measure of risk is represented by a different letter of the Greek alphabet:

DELTA - Δ

Delta (Δ) represents the rate of change between the option's price and the underlying asset's price - in other words, price sensitivity.

Delta is one of the most important Greeks. It tells us four different and important things about our position:

1. It's simply a change in the option's price relative to a change in the underlying stock or index price, when all other factors are

held constant. In other words, delta is the rate of change in an option's theoretical value for each one unit change in the underlying stock or index price.

2. Delta can also help as a determination of the probability of an option finishing ITM. This is useful if we do not have access to a trading platform that shows probability of expiring. For example, a call with a delta of 0.3 will have an approximate probability of finishing ITM of about 30%.

3. Delta also indicates whether you are bullish or bearish. If your deltas are positive, you want the underlying to go up. If your deltas are negative, you want the underlying to go down.

4. Delta also approximates the number of stock shares your position emulates. If you have a delta of 0.50, your position typically performs like 50 shares of stock (0.50 x 100 shares per contract = 50).

Purchased or Long Calls have positive delta, between 0 and 1. That means if the stock price goes up and no other pricing variables change, the price for the call will go up. Here's an example. If a call has a delta of 0.50 and the stock goes up $1, in theory, the price of the call will go up about $0.50. If the stock goes down $1, in theory, the price of the call will go down about $0.50.

Purchased or Long Puts have a negative delta, between 0 and -1. That means if the stock goes up and no other pricing variables change, the price of the option will go down. For example, if a put has a delta of -0.50 and the stock goes up $1, in theory the price of the put will go down $0.50. If the stock goes down $1, in theory, the price of the put will go up $0.50.

TIP
The delta of a long call is positive, and the delta of a long put is negative. Delta is reversed for short calls and puts. Simply stated, a long call makes money when the stock's price increases, and a long put makes money when the stock's price decreases.

As a general rule, ITM options will move more than OTM options, and short-term options will react more than longer-term options to the same price change in the stock.

As expiration nears, the delta for ITM calls will approach 1, reflecting a one-to-one reaction to price changes in the stock. Delta for OTM calls will approach 0, and won't react at all to price changes in the stock. That's because if they are held until expiration, calls will either be exercised and "become stock" or they will expire worthless, and become nothing at all.

As an option gets further ITM, the probability it will be ITM at expiration increases as well. So the option's delta will increase. As an option gets further OTM, the probability it will be ITM at expiration decreases. So the option's delta will decrease.

THETA - Θ

Theta (Θ) measures the daily whittling down of an option's value due to time decay. Time deterioration is inescapable, and theta impacts option premium values seven days a week, 365 days a year.

Time decay is enemy number one for the option buyer. On the other hand, it's usually the option seller's best friend. Theta is the amount by which the price of calls and puts will decrease (at least in theory) for a one-day change in the time to expiration.

Long calls and puts have negative theta, and they lose money as time passes. If your option theta is 0.09, then you theoretically lose 9¢ per day on a long option.

Short calls and puts have positive theta, and make money as time passes. If your short call or put has a +0.07 theta, then you theoretically gain 7¢ per day on a short option.

Long term options tend to have a small theta, because they are not subject to as much immediate time decay as short term options.

Theta is also highest for ATM strike prices and slopes off towards zero for ITM and OTM options, responding to the passage of time and volatility changes in the same way as gamma. Typically, a highly volatile stock has greater theta than a less volatile stock.

TIP

As options traders, we "always" want to have positions that generate positive THETA. Together with Delta, gamma are the two Greeks most used by traders when analyzing their positions.

GAMMA - Γ

Gamma (Γ) is a Greek that measures how fast the delta changes in relation to changes in the underlying stock's price.

Simply put, Gamma is the rate that delta will change based on a $1 change in the stock price. So if delta is the "speed" at which option prices change, you can think of gamma as the "acceleration". So options with the highest gamma are the most responsive to changes in the price of the underlying stock.

For long calls or puts, gamma is always positive. For short options, gamma is always negative.

Gamma is highest for an ATM strike price, and slopes off towards zero for ITM and OTM strike prices. A good way to interpret gamma is to remember that long gamma "manufactures" delta in the direction the stock is moving. So positive gamma is why long calls receive more positive delta when the stock price rises, and why long puts receive more negative delta when the stock price falls. It is also why short gamma can be dangerous. If you speculate incorrectly on the direction of price movement, short gamma intensifies the pain.

If you are bullish and think a stock's price will move a great deal very quickly, then an option with relatively high gamma may be desirable. High positive gamma increases your delta if the stock's price moves favorably and, as noted above, it reduces your delta if the stock's price moves against you.

So what this boils down to is that the price of near-term ATM options will exhibit the most explosive response to price changes in the stock.

VEGA - Υ

Vega – (Υ) Don't let anyone tell you differently: Vega is not a Greek letter. So why is it a Greek? No one really knows. Seriously, vega is the theoretical amount that call and put prices will change for a corresponding one-point change in implied volatility.

Vega does not have any effect on the intrinsic value of options; it only affects the "time value" of an option's price.

The more time until expiration, the higher an option's vega. Vega also responds to changes in a stock's price relative to the option's strike price. Like gamma and theta, vega is highest for ATM options and lower for OTM and ITM options. This means that ATM options containing plenty of time before expiration are the most sensitive to implied volatility changes.

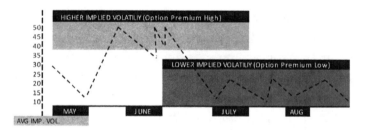

WE HAVE TO MENTION RHO - ρ

Rho (ρ) is the amount an option value will change in theory, based on a one percentage-point change in interest rates.

Just keep in mind that if you are trading shorter-term options, changing interest rates shouldn't affect the value of your options too much. But if you are trading long-term options such as leaps, rho can have a much more significant effect, due to greater "cost to carry".

USING THE GREEKS

Each Greek individually impacts your decision when buying and selling options. Evaluate the Greeks as a whole, because they may dramatically influence the success of your option strategy.

Stock price movement, time and volatility are three main factors that influence an option's price. With this knowledge of the Greeks, you can better understand and predict how an option's price is likely to respond to changes in any or all of these factors.

THE GREEKS AND HOW THEY AFFECT YOUR POSITIONS

- If the net <u>delta</u> of your position is <u>positive</u>, you want the underlying to rise.
- If the net <u>delta</u> of your position is <u>negative</u>, you want the underlying to fall.

- If the net <u>gamma</u> of your position is <u>positive</u>, you want the underlying to move rapidly (up or down).
- If the net <u>gamma</u> of your position is <u>negative</u>, you want the underlying to move slowly (up or down).

- If the net <u>theta</u> of your position is <u>positive</u>, time decay will benefit you.
- If the net <u>theta</u> of your position is <u>negative</u>, time decay will hurt you.

- If the net <u>vega</u> of your position is <u>positive</u>, you want volatility to rise.
- If the net <u>vega</u> of your position is <u>negative</u>, you want volatility to fall.

POSITION SIZING &
NUMBER OF TRADES

There are two things every investor should do before entering a trade: establish position size and define maximum portfolio risk.

Position sizing determines how much of your account is at risk in one trade. You should strive to keep individual position size (number of shares/contracts) at no more than 1-2% of your total portfolio value.

TRADE RISK

Trade Risk = the dollar amount at risk in your trade.

For example, if you have a $2.00 dollar wide spread when you paid $1.00 for the trade, your trade risk will be $1.00 or equal to your maximum loss.

Trade risk is also known as **buying power reduction**. It is the amount of capital your brokerage provider takes as collateral from your account, derived from an estimation of the amount of risk you are taking in a specific trade. Buying power reduction is different for every different type of brokerage account including:

- Cash Accounts
- IRA Accounts
- Margin Accounts
- Portfolio Margin Accounts.

The key is discipline. Commit yourself to consistently maintaining an appropriate position size for a risk level you have determined is appropriate for your portfolio, whether that is 1%, 2% or some other value. Apply the same position sizing rules to every trade. As you become more advanced, you will slightly tweak your position size depending on the type of strategy used. For example, you will use a much smaller trade size for a naked strangle with undefined risk than for a defined risk trade such as an Iron Condor.

If you did not understand the last paragraph, don't worry! It will all be clear to you when we learn each of the individual strategies will use to construct our overall portfolio.

TOTAL PORTFOLIO RISK

Total Portfolio Risk = the dollar amount at risk in your portfolio.

For example, if you have a $100,000 account and you risk 1 percent in seven different trades, the total portfolio risk is $7,000 ($100,000 x 7% = $7,000).

You never want to use all of your trading capital, in case something goes wrong. As a rule of thumb, a new trader must start by using between 5% and 25% of their trading portfolio. A more advanced trader can increase their total portfolio risk to around 75%. It is always important to have extra capital to hand, in case you need to make any adjustments to your positions or take advantage of a new opportunity that may come your way.

If you don't manage your total portfolio risk correctly, you could be victims of the dreaded MARGIN CALL. You receive a margin call from a broker if one or more of the securities you bought (with borrowed money) decreases in value past a certain point. You would be forced to either deposit more money in the account or to sell off some of your assets.

You must try to control position size at order entry as a "risk management tool". As strategy-based traders, we often need to give our positions time in order for them to go our way. If your position size is small you can wait out the trade, allowing duration to help you "be right", but if your position size is too big and the trade starts going against you, you will probably won't have the internal fortitude to wait out the position and allow it to go your way.

Since all of your trades will be probability based, it is important to have as many different trades possible in your portfolio. For example, we know that flipping a coin has a 50/50 probability of success. If you do 10 coin flips there is a chance, even if it's a small chance, that we could get 10 heads or 10 tails. But if you do 1,000 coins flips, the likelihood of having all of them end all heads or all tails is considerably reduced.

So in order to place the odds on your side, you need to:

1. trade small and
2. trade as often as possible.

BROKERAGE ACCOUNTS AND OPTION TRADING

Many traders are confused about how their option trading is affected by the type of account they have. There are three different types of brokerage accounts. They are:

- Cash Accounts
- Margin Accounts
- Retirement Accounts.

In order to trade options in any of these accounts, you must first be approved for options trading.

Approval for options trading is based on your experience. Your broker will typically ask how many years' experience you have trading options. In your account application you are usually asked what types of options trading you have done. Have you only bought options? Have you done spreads? Have you written naked options?

CASH ACCOUNTS

In a cash account, you will only be able to execute option trades on a cash basis. If you only plan to buy options this is usually not too much of a constraint. Purchasing options is always done on a cash basis even in a margin account, so there is nothing lost by buying an option in a cash account. However, your broker will require a cash deposit if you write options. Usually this is too onerous a requirement to make any reasonable return on option writing.

You may also be able to write covered calls in a cash account. You do have to put up the money for the stock, but can sell the call with no additional investment required.

MARGIN ACCOUNTS

In a margin account, you can borrow money by putting up the stock as collateral. However when you buy an option, you must put up the entire cash price of the option at the time of purchase. This is just the same as buying an option in a cash account.

The main advantage of trading options in a margin account is that most brokers allow you to put up a much smaller margin deposit, which gives you a better return on investment. Remember, for all practical purposes your investment is your margin deposit. So the relevant metric is the return on margin.

As an example, consider selling a put with a 25 strike price. Assuming the stock is more than 10% away from the money, your margin at many brokers will be $250 or 10% of the strike price. Compare that to putting up $2500 in a cash or retirement account for the same trade. Clearly the margin account is the better way to go.

RETIREMENT ACCOUNTS

I am loosely including all types of retirement accounts in this category. The account could be an IRA, Roth IRA, Rollover IRA, 401K or other retirement accounts. Usually the brokers are stricter with option margin requirements, simply because of their legal liability. You can usually only sell an option on a cash basis or as a covered call. You cannot even do an option spread at some brokers.

In most cases, retirement accounts will be treated as a cash account. In some IRA accounts you do have a bit of margin, but normally they are treated as cash accounts.

In order to trade more than 3 times a week, you need to have more than $25,000 USD in your account.

The primary difference with IRA and regular investing is that the trustees from the brokerage firms insist on very strict rules for people to trade. Those trustees put certain guidelines on risk.

In order to be successful in trading on an IRA account, people need to have the ability to use several strategies. The two most popular strategies done in an IRA are the Covered Call, and the Naked Put.

Naked call selling is normally not allowed in retirement accounts, eliminating high probability trades like naked strangles. Again, all this will be explained later.

PORTFOLIO MARGIN

In the discussion on margin accounts above, I used an example based on <u>Reg. T Margin</u>. However, there is another type of margin called portfolio margin you can often choose. The exact computation is a little tricky, and it is something not all brokers have chosen to offer. The computation is based on the volatility of your portfolio, and takes into account how diversified your portfolio is. It will often reduce your margin requirements, if you maintain a diversified portfolio with a significant number of positions, however, it is only available to margin accounts.

Portfolio margin is available for traders that can pass a portfolio margin test, and have an account with a minimum of $125,000 dollars. This type of account will generally give you three times more leverage than a regular margin account.

Previously, portfolio margin requirements used to be $5,000,000 because they were only offered to Institutional Investors. Now the minimum is much less, at $125,000.

The main difference between margin and portfolio margin (PM) are:

1. For Stocks trades, PM gives you 2/1 overnight.
2. For Intraday stock purchases, PM gives you 4/1.
3. On Naked Options, your PM goes up to 6/1.

4. A great additional benefit of PM is that it allows offsetting positions on long/short stocks, options and futures. So recognized pairs help you reduce your risk, increasing your margin.

READY FOR THE STRATEGIES?

Now that we have learned the basic trading terminology, we can start focusing on the good stuff - the strategies.

The keys to consistently making money in the markets lies with the correct selection and implementation of strategies, trade size and trade quantity. Being right "directionally" is important, but selecting the correct strategy will still allow you to be slightly wrong in your directional assumption and yet still make money. It will also allow you to wait out your position in order to be right.

THE STRATEGIES

Trading stocks, be it long or short, has a probability of success of 50%. That is right; even if you have analyzed all the fundamental and technical aspects of the underlying, every time that you place a stock trade it still has only a 50% probability of profit in the next 30 days.

The concept of "unlimited" profits is one of the main reasons people buy stocks, but you will learn that unlimited profits have a very, very small probability of happening.

You will also learn that whenever you limit your profitability, you will automatically increase your probability of profit for a specific trade.

That is the one of the keys of profitable trading; limiting your profitability in exchange for a higher chance to make money. So here are the strategies in detail.

STRATEGY # 1
COVERED CALL WRITING

Many investors use covered calls as a first foray into option trading, probably because they are easy to understand and execute.

DEFINITION
Covered call writing is the simultaneous purchase of stock and sale of a call option against the stock position. Generally, one call option is sold for every 100 shares of stock.

DIRECTIONAL ASSUMPTION
This is a bullish trade, meaning that you will benefit if the price of the stock rises during the life of the trade.

TRADE EXAMPLE
Long 100 shares of IBM at $100, and sell one $110 strike call with 30 days left for $2.50.

MAXIMUM GAIN
Strike Price of the Option minus Stock Purchase Price plus Premium Received.

In this example, ($110.00 - $100.00) + $2.50 = Maximum gain for $12.50.

MAXIMUM LOSS

Stock Purchase Price minus Premium Received.

In this example, $100 - $2.50 = $97.50.
Theoretically the stock could go down to zero, so you could potentially lose the full invested amount of $97.50.

BREAK EVEN

Stock Purchase Price minus Premium Received.

In this example, $100.00 - $2.50 = $97.50.

THE MECHANICS

1. Choose a stock in your portfolio that is "liquid" and that has at least the same implied volatility as the SPY or SPX. Or, choose a completely new stock that you feel has an opportunity to go up.
2. Find the nearest OTM call that has at least 20 days to expiration and no longer than 60 days.
3. Or pick a call strike price which you'd be comfortable selling the stock at. The goal is for the stock to rise further in price before you'll have to sell it.
4. As a general rule of thumb, some investors think about 2% to 3% of the stock value is an acceptable premium to look for. Remember, with options, time is money. The further out in time you go, the more an option will be worth. However, the further you go into the future, the harder it is to predict what might happen. Beware of receiving too much time value. If the premium seems abnormally high, there's usually a reason for it! Check for news in the marketplace that may affect the price of the stock, and remember if something seems too good to be true, it usually is.

POSSIBLE OUTCOMES

There are three possible outcomes for this play:

Outcome # 1 - The stock goes down

If the stock price is down at the time the option expires, the good news is that your call will expire worthless, and you'll keep the entire premium received for selling it. Obviously, the bad news is that the value of the stock is down. That's the nature of a covered call. The risk comes from owning the stock. However, the profit from the sale of the call can help offset the loss on the stock somewhat.

Outcome # 2: the stock stays at the same price or goes up a little, but does not reach the strike price

There's really no bad news in this scenario, and in fact, it may be the best scenario. The call option you sold will expire worthless, so you pocket the entire premium from selling it, and perhaps you've even seen some gains on the underlying stock, which you will still own. You can't complain about that.

Outcome # 3: The stock rises above the strike price

If the stock is above the strike price at expiration, the call option will be assigned, and you'll have to sell 100 shares of the stock.

If the stock skyrockets after you sell the shares, you might consider kicking yourself for missing out on any additional gains, but don't. You made a conscious decision that you were willing to sell the stock at the strike price, and you achieved the maximum profit potential from the play.

THINGS TO REMEMBER

The risk in this trade comes primarily from owning the stock – not from selling the call. The sale of the option only limits opportunity on the upside, and it also increases your probability of success.

When doing a covered call, you're taking advantage of time decay on the options you sold. Every day the stock doesn't move, the call you sold will decline in value, which benefits you as the seller.

As long as the stock price doesn't reach the strike price, your stock won't get called away. So in theory, you can repeat this strategy indefinitely on the same lot of stock.

TRADE SUMMARY

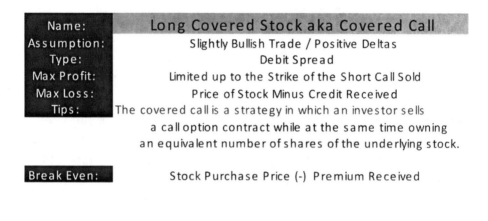

Name:	Long Covered Stock aka Covered Call
Assumption:	Slightly Bullish Trade / Positive Deltas
Type:	Debit Spread
Max Profit:	Limited up to the Strike of the Short Call Sold
Max Loss:	Price of Stock Minus Credit Received
Tips:	The covered call is a strategy in which an investor sells a call option contract while at the same time owning an equivalent number of shares of the underlying stock.
Break Even:	Stock Purchase Price (-) Premium Received

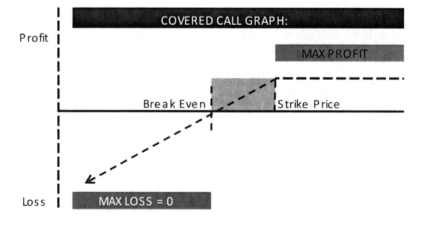

COVERED CALL GRAPH:

Profit

MAX PROFIT

Break Even Strike Price

Loss MAX LOSS = 0

STRATEGY # 2
LONG CALL

Options trading is more complicated than trading stock, and for a first-timer, it can be scary. That is why many investors decide to begin trading options by buying short term calls. Especially OTM (out of the money), meaning the strike price is above the current stock price. But take note – Long Calls are rarely used by Tom and Tony.

DEFINITION
Buying a long call gives you the right to buy the underlying stock at strike price "X". A long call is simply purchasing a call on a stock that you are bullish on, buying it either ATM, ITM or OTM.

In general, the more OTM the call is, the more bullish the strategy, as bigger increases in the underlying stock price are required for the option to reach the breakeven point.

DIRECTIONAL ASSUMPTION
This is a bullish trade, meaning that you will benefit if the price of the stock rises during the life of the trade. The problem here is that in order to make money, you need the stock to go to your strike price plus the premium paid for the call in order to make money. This is a NEGATIVE THETA trade, with a low probability of success.

TRADE EXAMPLE
IBM now trading at $100, and you decide to buy the $110 strike call with 30 days left for $2.50.

MAXIMUM GAIN
There's a theoretically unlimited profit potential, but I am sorry, I have never seen this happen.

In this example, this will happen after your stock goes past $112.50.

MAXIMUM LOSS
Limited to the Premium Paid.

In this example, $2.50 would be your max loss, and this will happen if IBM is trading below $110 at expiration.

BREAK EVEN
Strike Price plus Premium Paid

In this example, $110 + $2.50 = $112.50

LONG CALLS AS STOCK SUBSTITUTES
Calls may be used as an alternative to buying stock outright. You can profit if the stock rises, without taking on all of the downside risk that would result from owning the stock. It is also possible to gain leverage over a greater number of shares that you could afford to buy outright, because calls are always less expensive than the stock itself.

But be careful, especially with short-term OTM calls. If you buy too many option contracts, you are actually increasing your risk. Options may expire worthless, and you can lose your entire investment, whereas if you own the stock it will usually still be worth something.

While holding the call option, the investor retains the right to purchase an equivalent number of underlying shares at the predetermined strike price at any time until the contract expires.

VOLATILITY

- If Volatility Increases: Positive Effect
- If Volatility Decreases: Negative Effect

Any effect of volatility on the option's total premium is on the time value portion.

THETA

Passage of Time: Negative Effect

The time value portion of an option's premium, which the option holder has "purchased" by paying for the option, generally decreases or decays with the passage of time. This decrease accelerates as the option contract approaches expiration.

TIPS

1. If you do decide to purchase a call, you may wish to consider buying the contract ITM, since it's likely to have a larger delta (that is, changes in the option's value will correspond more closely with any change in the stock price).
2. Try looking for a delta of 0.70 or 0.80 or greater if possible.
3. ITM options are more expensive because they have intrinsic value, but you get a higher probability of profit.

TRADE SUMMARY

Name:	Long Call
Assumption:	Bullish Trade / Positive Deltas
Type:	Debit Paid
Max Profit:	Unlimited
Max Loss:	Debit Paid
Tips:	Low probability trade
	Negative Theta
	Buy a Call with 70% or 80% Prob of Expiring
	Buy 20 to 90 days out
Break Even:	Strike Price (+) Premium paid

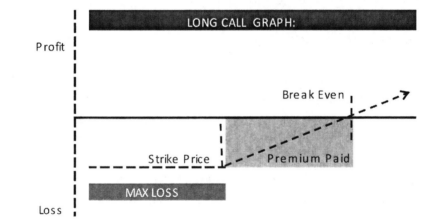

STRATEGY # 3

LONG PUT

Long puts are also rarely used by Tom and Tony.

DEFINITION

A long put gives you the right to sell the underlying stock at strike price "X".

If there were no such thing as puts, the only way to benefit from a downward movement in the market would be to sell stock short. The problem with shorting stock is that you're exposed to theoretically un-limited risk if the stock price rises.

But when you use puts as an alternative to short stock, your risk is limited to the cost of the option contracts. If the stock goes up (the worst-case scenario), you don't have to buy back shares as you would with short stock. You simply allow your puts to expire worthless or sell them to close your position (if they're still worth anything).

DIRECTIONAL ASSUMPTION

This is a bearish trade, meaning that you will benefit if the price of the stock falls during the life of the trade. The problem here is that in order to make money, you need the stock to fall past your strike price plus the premium paid for the put. This is a NEGATIVE THETA trade, with a low probability of success.

TRADE EXAMPLE
IBM is now trading at $100.00 and you decide to buy the $90.00 strike put with 30 days left for $3.00.

MAXIMUM GAIN
There's a theoretically unlimited profit potential, although stocks can only go to zero (thankfully)!

MAXIMUM LOSS
Maximum loss is limited to the Premium Paid.

In this example, $3.00 would be your max loss, and this will happen if IBM is trading above $90 at expiration.

BREAK EVEN
Strike Price minus Premium Paid.

In this example, $90.00 - $3.00 = $87.00
Be careful here, because at expiration you will not make a profit if the stock is not below $87.00.

LONG PUTS AS SHORT STOCK SUBSTITUTES
Puts may be used as an alternative to shorting stock outright. You can profit if the stock falls, without taking on all of the upside risk that would result from owning the stock. It is also possible to gain leverage over a greater number of shares than you could afford to sell outright, because puts are always less expensive than the stock itself.

While holding the put option, the investor retains the right to sell an equivalent number of underlying shares at the predetermined strike price at any time until the contract expires.

VOLATILITY
- If Volatility Increases: Positive Effect
- If Volatility Decreases: Negative Effect

Any effect of volatility on the option's total premium is on the time value portion.

THETA

Passage of Time: Negative Effect

The time value portion of an option's premium, which the option holder has "purchased" by paying for the option, generally decreases, or decays, with the passage of time. This decrease accelerates as the option contract approaches expiration.

TIPS

1. If you do decide to purchase a put, you may wish to consider buying an ITM put, since it's likely to have a greater delta (that is, changes in the options' value will correspond more closely with any change in the stock price).
2. Try looking for a delta of 0.70 or 0.80 or greater if possible.
3. ITM options are more expensive because they have intrinsic value, but you get what you pay for.

TRADE SUMMARY

Name:	Long Put
Assumption:	Bearish Trade / Negative Deltas
Type:	Debit paid
Max Profit:	Up to Zero
Max Loss:	Debit paid
Tips:	Low probability trade
	Negative Theta
	Buy a Putt with 70% to 80% Prob of Expiring
	Buy 20 to 90 days out
Break Even:	Strike Price (-) Premium paid

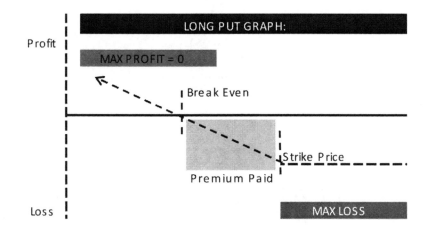

STRATEGY # 4
COVERED PUT WRITING

This trade is exactly the same as a covered call, but the main difference is that it is using puts instead of calls. For me, as for many other investors, it was hard at the beginning of my trading career to focus on the downside instead of the upside. Humans are wired to always think of the upside, and the concept of profiting from a down move or selling something we do not own takes a little practice and getting used to.

Once you get the hang of this trade, it will both help round up your trading knowledge and also help you balance your portfolio deltas.

DEFINITION
Covered put writing is the simultaneous sale of stock and the sale of a put option against the stock position. Generally one put option is sold for every 100 shares of stock.

DIRECTIONAL ASSUMPTION
This is a bearish trade, meaning that you will benefit if the price of the stock falls during the life of the trade.

TRADE EXAMPLE
Short 100 shares of IBM at $100, and sell one $90 strike put with 30 days left for $2.50.

MAXIMUM GAIN

Short Stock Sale Price minus Strike Price of the Option Sold plus Premium Received.

In this example, ($100.00-$90-00) + $2.50 = Maximum gain for $12.50

BREAK EVEN

Short Stock Sale Price plus Premium Received.

In this example, $100 + $2.50 = $102.50.

MAXIMUM LOSS

Any price above the Short Stock Sale Price plus Premium Received.

In this example, $100 + $2.50 = $102.50. Theoretically the stock could go up indefinitely, and you would start to lose after your breakeven point is passed.

THE MECHANICS

1. Choose a stock in your portfolio that is "liquid" and that has at least the same implied volatility as the SPY or SPX. Or choose a completely new stock that you feel has an opportunity to go down.
2. Find the nearest OTM put that has at least 20 days to expiration and no longer than 60 days.
3. Or pick a put strike price of which you'd be comfortable buying the stock at. The goal is for the stock to fall further in price before you'll have to cover it.
4. As a general rule of thumb, some investors think around 2% to 3% of the stock value is an acceptable premium to look for. Remember, with options, time is money. The further you go out in time, the more an option will be worth. However, the further you go into the future, the harder it is to predict what might

happen. Beware of receiving too much time value. If the premium seems abnormally high, there's usually a reason for it. Check for news in the marketplace that may affect the price of the stock, and remember if something seems too good to be true, it usually is.

TIPS
1. Since you are short the stock, you will be responsible for the dividends paid for the stock.
2. Always make sure you cover your short stock positions before the ex-dividend date, so you can avoid the very unpleasant experience of having to pay a dividend on a stock you do not own.

POSSIBLE OUTCOMES
There are three possible outcomes for this play:

Outcome # 1: The stock goes up
If the stock price is up at the time the option expires, the good news is the put will expire worthless, and you'll keep the entire premium received for selling it. Obviously, the bad news is that the value of the stock is up, and you are losing money because you are short. That's the nature of a covered put. The risk comes from selling or shorting the stock. However, the profit from the sale of the put can help offset the loss on the stock somewhat.

Outcome # 2: The stock stays at the same price or goes down a little, but does not reach the strike price
There's really no bad news in this scenario. In fact, it may be the best scenario. The put option you sold will expire worthless, so you pocket the entire premium from selling it. Perhaps you've seen some gains on the underlying stock, which you will be short. You can't complain about that.

Outcome # 3: The stock falls below the strike price

If the stock is below the strike price at expiration, the call option will be assigned, and you'll have to buy back your 100 shares of the stock.

If the stock plummets after you buy back the shares, you might consider kicking yourself for missing out on any additional gains, but don't. You made a conscious decision that you were willing to buy back the stock at the strike price, and you achieved the maximum profit potential from the play.

THINGS TO REMEMBER

The risk in this trade comes primarily from being short a stock you don't own – not from selling the put. The sale of the option only limits opportunity on the downside but also increases your probability of success. Also don't forget about dividend risk. Normally Index ETF like SPY, and QQQ pay go ex-dividend on regular option expiration every quarter, make sure you cover your positions at least one day before.

When doing a covered put, you're taking advantage of time decay on the options you sold. Every day the stock doesn't move, the put you sold will decline in value, which benefits you as the seller.

As long as the stock price doesn't reach the strike price, your short stock won't get called away. So in theory, you can repeat this strategy indefinitely on the same lot of stock.

TRADE SUMMARY

Name:	Short Covered Stock or Covered Put
Assumption:	Slightly Bearish Trade / negative Deltas
Type:	Credit Spread
Max Profit:	Limited up to the Strike of the Short Putt Sold
Max Loss:	Price of Shorted Stock Plus Credit Received
Tips:	The covered put is a strategy in which an investor sells a putt option contract while at the same time shorting an equivalent number of shares of the underlying stock.
Break Even:	Stock Shorted Price (+) Premium Received

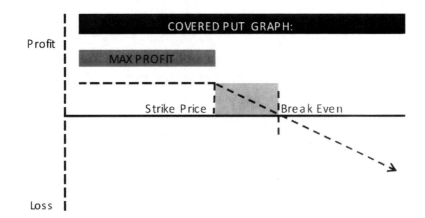

STRATEGY # 5

SHORT CALL

(aka NAKED CALL)

DEFINITION

An uncovered short call is selling a call on a stock you don't own.

DIRECTIONAL ASSUMPTION

This is a bearish trade, meaning that you will benefit if the price of the stock is below your strike price at expiration.

Selling the call obligates you to sell stock at strike price "X" if the option is assigned.

When doing this trade, you want the call you sell to expire worthless. That's why most investors sell OTM options.

This play has a limited profit potential (premium received for selling the call), if the stock remains below strike "X" at expiration, but also unlimited potential risk if the stock goes up. The reason some traders do this trade is that there is a high probability for success when selling OTM options.

TRADE EXAMPLE

IBM is now trading at $100 and you decide to sell one $110 strike call with 30 days left for $2.50.

MAXIMUM GAIN

Potential profit is limited to the Premium Received for selling the call.

In this example, $2.50.

MAXIMUM LOSS

Risk is theoretically unlimited. If the stock keeps rising above your sold strike "X", you keep losing money.

BREAK EVEN

Strike Price plus Premium Received.

In this example, $110.00 + $2.50 = $112.50.

VOLATILITY

After the play is established, you want implied volatility to decrease.

- If Volatility Increases: Negative Effect
- If Volatility Decreases: Positive Effect

THETA

Passage of Time: Positive

The time value portion of an option's premium, which the option holder has "collected" by selling the option, generally increases with the passage of time. Theta normally accelerates as the option contract approaches expiration.

TIPS

1. You may wish to consider selecting a strike when "X" is around one standard deviation of OTM at initiation. That will increase your probability of success. However, the higher the strike price, the lower the premium received from this play.

2. Also, never do this play on stocks that might be taken over or on the $VIX, because in both cases the risk is to the upside, and this is risk you cannot control or recover from.
3. This type of trade is only suited for the most advanced option traders, because it has potentially unlimited risk to the upside.

TRADE SUMMARY

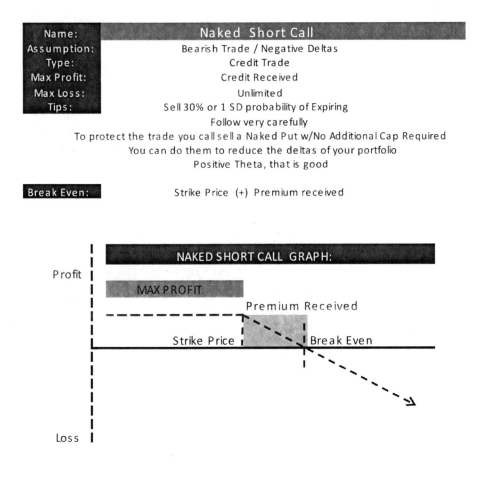

Name:	Naked Short Call
Assumption:	Bearish Trade / Negative Deltas
Type:	Credit Trade
Max Profit:	Credit Received
Max Loss:	Unlimited
Tips:	Sell 30% or 1 SD probability of Expiring
	Follow very carefully
	To protect the trade you call sell a Naked Put w/No Additional Cap Required
	You can do them to reduce the deltas of your portfolio
	Positive Theta, that is good
Break Even:	Strike Price (+) Premium received

STRATEGY # 6
SHORT PUT
(aka NAKED PUT)

What if you could buy stocks for less than the current market price? And what if you could make money when you are wrong about the direction of the market? If either of those two scenarios sounds appealing to you, then you perhaps should consider selling naked puts.

This trade is very similar to a covered call, in fact if you look at the risk graphs of both trades, they are practically identical. The main differences are that the covered call requires more capital, and the naked put has a higher probability of success if sold OTM.

DEFINITION
An uncovered short put is selling a put on a stock you don't own.

DIRECTIONAL ASSUMPTION
This is a bullish trade, meaning that you will benefit if the price of the stock is above your strike price at expiration.

Selling the put obligates you to buy stock at strike price "X" if the option is assigned.

When doing this trade, you want the put you sell to expire worthless. That's why most investors sell OTM options.

This play has a limited profit potential (premium received for selling the put), if the stock remains above strike "X" at expiration, but unlimited potential risk if the stock goes down.

TRADE EXAMPLE
IBM is now trading at $100 and you decide to sell the $90 strike put with 30 days left for $3.00.

MAXIMUM GAIN
Potential Profit is limited to the Premium Received for selling the put.

In this example, $3.00

MAXIMUM LOSS
Risk is theoretically very big. If the stock goes below your strike of "X", you keep losing money. The good thing is that stocks only go to Zero, so $0.00 would be your max loss.

BREAK EVEN
Strike Price minus Premium Received.

In this example, $90.00 - $3.00 = $87.00.

VOLATILITY
After the play is established, you want implied volatility to decrease.

- If Volatility Increases: Negative Effect
- If Volatility Decreases: Positive Effect

THETA
Passage of Time: Positive

The time value portion of an option's premium, which the option holder has "collected" by selling the option, generally increases with the passage of time. Theta normally accelerates as the option contract approaches expiration.

TIPS

1. You may wish to consider selecting a strike "X" of around one standard deviation from OTM at initiation. That will increase your probability of success. However the lower the strike price, the lower the premium received from this play.
2. This type of trade is only suited for the most advanced option traders, because it has potentially unlimited risk to the downside.

TRADE SUMMARY

Name:	Naked Short Put
Assumption:	Bullish Trade / Positive Deltas
Type:	Credit Trade
Max Profit:	Credit Received
Max Loss:	Up to Zero
Tips:	Sell 30% or 1 SD probability of Expiring
	Follow very carefully
	To protect the trade you call sell a Naked Call w/No Additional Cap Require
	Only do them for adjustment of Deltas
	Positive Theta, that is good
	Do them if you are willing to buy the stock at
	your sold strike.
Break Even:	Strike Price (-) Premium received

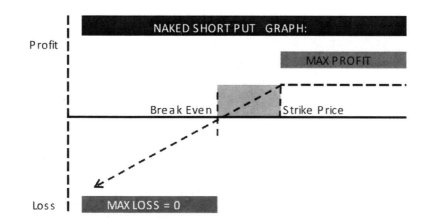

VERTICAL SPREADS

Two strategies serve as the foundation to most trading strategies: verticals and calendars.

Vertical spreads are very common strategies employed by retail and professional traders alike. Understanding verticals is vital for trading other strategies like butterflies, iron condors, and diagonals, to name just a few. Understanding the ins and outs of verticals makes it much easier for you to understand other strategies taught later in this book.

Vertical spreads can be divided in two main groups:
- Long Vertical Spreads
- Short Vertical Spreads.

Long Vertical Spreads can also be divided into two groups:
- Long Call Verticals, aka Bull Call spreads
- Long Put Verticals, aka Bear Put Spreads.

Short Vertical Spreads can also divide into two groups:
- Short Call Verticals, aka Bear Call spreads
- Short Put Verticals, aka Bull Put Spreads.

The cool thing about vertical spreads is that they allow you to be slightly wrong in your direction assumption, and still make money.

STRATEGY # 7
LONG CALL VERTICAL
(aka BULL CALL SPREAD)

Many professional investors use long vertical spread strategies when making directional trades with option contracts. Professionals seldom buy naked options, due to their low probability of success, preferring to protect their positions through the use of spread trades. A long vertical spread is a better choice because it offers reduced risk and requires smaller moves in the underlying stock to achieve profits.

DEFINITION
A long call vertical is the simultaneous purchase of a lower strike price call and sale of a higher strike price call, with the same expiration month.

DIRECTIONAL ASSUMPTION
This is a bullish trade, meaning that you will benefit if the price of the stock is at or above your short strike price at expiration.

THE MECHANICS
You normally buy the first ITM option call and sell the first OTM call. You can still create time decay, while buying a debit spread.

PROBABILITY OF SUCCESS

This trade gives you approximately a 50% probability of success.

TIPS

1. You do Debit Spreads when you want a higher payout, as you can risk (one) to make (one).
2. Look for options with at least 20 days to expiration and no longer than 60 days.
3. For your short strike selection you can also pick a strike price that you might think the stock can go to. The goal is for the stock to rise to or past your short strike.

TRADE EXAMPLE

IBM is now trading at $97.00 and you decide to buy the $95 call and sell the $100.00 strike call in the same expiration month, for a net debit of $2.50.

MAXIMUM GAIN

Your maximum profit is the difference between a spread's two strike prices, minus the amount paid and commissions. Maximum profit for a long vertical call spread is realized when the stock moves at or above the higher strike price.

In this example, if IBM goes to $100 at expiration, our spread will be worth $5.00. Minus the $2.50 we paid for the spread, this will give us a profit of $2.50.

MAXIMUM LOSS

The maximum loss is the amount you pay for the spread, plus commissions. This occurs if the spread expires worthless, with the underlying stock at or below the strike price of the long call on expiration day.

In this example, this would happen if IBM is at or below $95 at expiration.

BREAK EVEN

The breakeven point at expiration of a long vertical call spread is equal to the Long Call Strike Price plus the Premium Paid, not including commissions.

In this example, $95.00 + $2.50 = $97.50.

CAPITAL REQUIRED OR BUYING POWER REDUCTION

The amount of buying power necessary to trade a long vertical spread is equal to the trade's cost or debit.

For example, if we bought our vertical spread for $2.50, your capital requirement is $250.00 per spread ($2.50 x 100 shares per contract = $250.00).

ADJUSTMENT

If you are lucky enough to be correct on your trade right away, you have two choices:
1. You can take your profit, and be happy
2. You can butterfly the position off, by selling a short option vertical on your short strike and with the same trade width as the original debit spread.

TIP: HOW TO TAKE A PROFITABLE LONG CREDIT SPREAD AND TURN IT INTO A FREE BUTTERFLY

Example: You Buy the SPY, JAN, 120-122 Long Call Vertical for $1.00.
Then SPY goes up, and your trade is a winner right away.
Now you can Butterfly the position by selling the 122-124 Short Call vertical, for $1.00 or better.

In this adjustment you want to collect the same or similar amount you paid for the long vertical in order to have a butterfly on for free.

TRADE SUMMARY

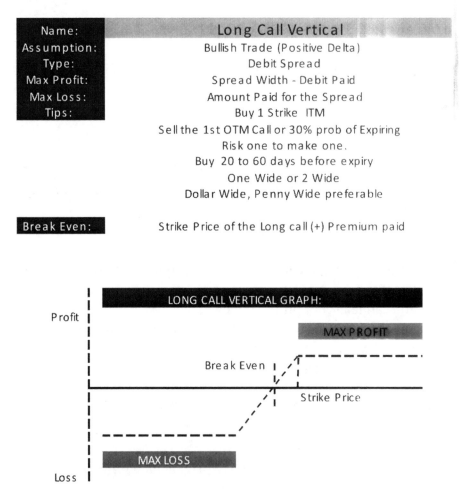

Name:	Long Call Vertical
Assumption:	Bullish Trade (Positive Delta)
Type:	Debit Spread
Max Profit:	Spread Width - Debit Paid
Max Loss:	Amount Paid for the Spread
Tips:	Buy 1 Strike ITM
	Sell the 1st OTM Call or 30% prob of Expiring
	Risk one to make one.
	Buy 20 to 60 days before expiry
	One Wide or 2 Wide
	Dollar Wide, Penny Wide preferable
Break Even:	Strike Price of the Long call (+) Premium paid

STRATEGY # 8
LONG PUT VERTICAL
(aka BEAR PUT SPREAD)

DEFINITION
A long put vertical is the simultaneous purchase of a higher strike price put and sale of a lower strike price put, with the same expiration month.

DIRECTIONAL ASSUMPTION
This is a bearish trade, meaning that you will benefit if the price of the stock is at or below your short strike price at expiration.

THE MECHANICS
You normally buy the first ITM option put and sell the first OTM put. You can still create time decay, while buying a debit spread.

PROBABILITY OF SUCCESS
This trade gives you approximately a 50% probability of success.

TIPS
1. You do Debit Spreads when you want a higher payout, as you can risk (one) to make (one).
2. Look for options with at least 20 days to expiration a no longer than 60 days.

3. For your short strike selection you can also pick a strike price that you might think the stock can go to. The goal is for the stock to fall to or past your short strike.

TRADE EXAMPLE

IBM is now trading at $97.00 and you decide to buy the $100 put, and sell the $95.00 strike put in the same expiration month, for a net debit of $2.50.

MAXIMUM GAIN

Your maximum profit is the difference between the spread's two strike prices, minus the amount paid plus commissions. Maximum profit for a long vertical put spread is realized when the stock moves at or below the lower strike price.

In the example, if IBM goes to $95.00 at expiration, your spread will be worth $5.00, minus the $2.50 you paid for the spread, giving you a profit of $2.50.

MAXIMUM LOSS

The maximum loss is the amount you pay for the spread, plus commissions. This occurs if the spread expires worthless, with the underlying stock at or above the strike price of the long put on expiration day.

In this example, this would occur if IBM is at or above $100 at expiration.

BREAK EVEN

The breakeven point at expiration of a long vertical put spread is equal to the long put strike price minus the premium paid, not including commissions.

In this example, $100.00 - $2.50 = $97.50.

CAPITAL REQUIRED OR BUYING POWER REDUCTION

The amount of buying power necessary to trade a long vertical spread is equal to the trade's cost or debit.

For example, if we bought our vertical spread for $2.50, your capital requirement is $250.00 per spread ($2.50 x 100 shares per contract = $250.00).

ADJUSTMENT

If you are lucky enough to be correct on your trade right away, you have two choices:
1. You can take your profit, and be happy.
2. You can butterfly the position off, by selling a short put vertical on your short strike and with the same trade width as the original debit spread.

TIP: HOW TO TAKE A PROFITABLE LONG CREDIT SPREAD INTO A FREE BUTTERFLY

Example: You Buy the SPY JAN, 122-120 Long Call Put for $1.00.
Then SPY goes down and your trade is a winner right away.
Now you can Butterfly the position by selling the 120-118 Short Put vertical, for $1.00 or better.

In this adjustment you want to collect the same or similar amount you paid for the long vertical in order to have a butterfly on for free.

TRADE SUMMARY

Name:	Long Put Vertical
Assumption:	Bearish Trade (Negative Delta)
Type:	Debit Spread
Max Profit:	Spread Width - Debit Paid
Max Loss:	Amount Paid for the Spread
Tips:	Buy 1 Strike ITM
	Sell the 1st OTM Putt or 30% prob of Expiring
	Risk one to make one.
	Buy 20 to 60 days before expiry
	One Wide or 2 Wide
	Dollar Wide, Penny Wide preferable
Break Even:	Strike Price of the Long Putt (-) Premium paid

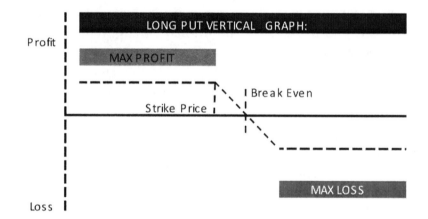

STRATEGY # 9

SHORT CALL VERTICAL

(aka BEAR CALL SPREAD)

DEFINITION

A short vertical call spread (Bear Call) is the sale of the lower strike call and purchase of the higher strike call with the same expiration month.

DIRECTIONAL ASSUMPTION

This is a bearish to neutral trade, meaning that you will benefit if the price of the stock is at or below your short strike price at expiration.

THE MECHANICS

Normally you want to collect at least 30% of the width of the strikes. That can sometimes be accomplished by selling the 30% probability of expiring strike or somewhere around that area.

PROBABILITY OF SUCCESS

This trade gives you an approximate 70% probability of success. You calculate the probability by simply subtracting the credit received from the width of the strike

TIPS

1. You normally do credit spreads instead of debit spreads when you want a higher probability of success in case you are wrong directionally, or in occasions where your conviction on market direction is not as strong.
2. Look for options with at least 20 days to expiration and no longer than 60 days.
3. For your short strike selection you can also pick a strike price that you think the stock might not get to. The goal is for the stock to stay below your short strike.

TRADE EXAMPLE

IBM is now trading at $97.00 and you decide to sell the $100 call and buy the $102.00 strike call in the same expiration month, for a net credit of $0.66.

MAXIMUM GAIN

Short vertical spreads are executed for credits, so the credit received when you first placed the trade is your maximum profit.

Maximum profit for a short call vertical is realized when the stock stays at or below the short strike price.

In this example, if IBM goes up to a maximum value of less than $100 at expiration, your spread will be worth $0.00, and you would collect the whole $0.66 cent credit.

MAXIMUM LOSS

The maximum loss is equal to the dollar value of the difference between the strike prices of the short call and long call, minus the credit received when selling the vertical spread.

Maximum loss occurs if the underlying price of the stock at expiration is higher than the long call's strike price.

In this example, this would occur if IBM is at or above $102 at expiration. $2.00 - $0.66 = $1.34 loss.

BREAK EVEN

The breakeven point is the strike price of the short call, plus the premium for which you sold the spread.

In this example, $100.00 + $0.66 = $100.66

CAPITAL REQUIRED OR BUYING POWER REDUCTION

The amount of buying power necessary to trade a short vertical spread is equal to the position's maximum loss.

For example, if we sold our two strike wide vertical spread for $0.66 ($2.00-$0.66), then your capital requirement is $134.00 per spread ($1.34 x 100 shares per contract = $134.00).

VOLATILITY

Because you are both buying and selling options in the same month with the same overall market volatility, the effects of volatility will be somewhat offset by the long and short options.

If implied volatility is high we will be able to sell this credit spread further OTM and still collect our credit of around 1/3 of the width of the strikes.

If implied volatility is lower, we would have to get closer to an ATM strike in order to collect our desired credit.

This is a Vega negative trade, so after the play is established, you want implied volatility to decrease.

- If Volatility Increases: Negative Effect
- If Volatility Decreases: Positive Effect

THETA

Passage of Time: Positive

For this type of trade, the net effect of time decay is positive. It will erode the value of the option you sold (good) but it will also erode the value of the option you bought (bad).

ADJUSTMENT

You normally do not adjust this defined risk type of trade, knowing that approximately 33% of these types of trades will be losers, and 66% of the winners.

However, there are two adjustments that you can make that require no additional capital.

1. You could do a short put spread in the same stock and the same expiration month, in order to collect some additional credit to offset the losses that you are experiencing. If you do decide to go this route, we recommend that you do your short put spread at around the 20 delta for your short strike. The amount of credit that you will receive will depend on how many days there are left to expiration, and the implied volatility at the time of your trade. Expect that the additional credit received will be much less than the original credit that you got when you put on the trade.

2. You could "roll" the trade to the next calendar month by purchasing or closing the current credit spread, and simultaneously selling the next month spread. You can do the same strikes that you currently have, or move one or two strikes up in order to get additional breathing space, but make sure that you do this roll for a net credit. You should not pay up for position rolls.

TRADE SUMMARY

Name:	Short Call Vertical
Assumption:	Bearish Trade (Negative Delta)
Type:	Credit Spread
Max Profit:	Max Profit Is the Total Credit Received
Max Loss:	Spread Width - Credit Received
Tips:	Sell 30% OTM probability of Expiring
	Collect a min. of 1/3 of Width of the Strikes
	Sell 20 to 60 days before expiry
	One Wide or 2 Wide are the most common.
	Dollar Wide, Penny Wide preferable
Break Even:	Strike Price of the Short Call (+) Premium Received

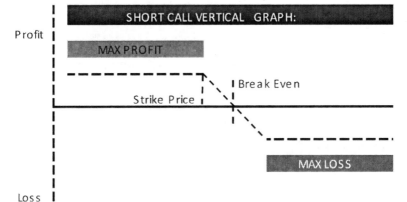

STRATEGY # 10
SHORT PUT VERTICAL
(aka BULL PUT SPREAD)

DEFINITION
A short vertical put spread (Bull Put) is the sale of a higher strike put and purchase of the lower strike put with the same expiration month.

DIRECTIONAL ASSUMPTION
This is a bullish to neutral trade, meaning that you will benefit if the price of the stock to be at or above your short strike price at expiration.

THE MECHANICS
Normally you want to collect at least 30% of the width of the strikes. That can sometimes be accomplished by selling the 30% probability of expiring strike or somewhere around that area.

PROBABILITY OF SUCCESS
This trade gives you approximately a 70% probability of success. You calculate the probability by simply subtracting the credit received from the width of the strike

TIPS

1. You normally do credit spreads instead of debit spreads when you want a higher probability of success in case you are wrong, or on occasions where your conviction on market direction is not as strong.
2. Look for options with at least 20 days to expiration and no longer than 60 days.
3. For your short strike selection you can also pick a strike price that you think the stock might not get to. The goal is for the stock to stay above your short strike.

TRADE EXAMPLE

IBM is now trading at $97.00 and you decide to sell the $95.00 put and buy the $93.00 strike put in the same expiration month for a net credit of $0.66.

MAXIMUM GAIN

Short vertical spreads are executed for credits, so the credit received when you first placed the trade is your maximum profit.

Maximum profit for a short put vertical is realized when the stock stays at or above the short strike price.

In this example, if IBM goes down to a value or above $95.00 at expiration, your spread will be worth $0.00. And you would collect the whole $0.66 cent credit.

MAXIMUM LOSS

The maximum loss is equal to the dollar value of the difference between the strike prices of the short put and long put, minus the credit received when selling the vertical spread.

Maximum loss occurs if the underlying price of the stock at expiration is lower than the long put strike price.

In this example this would occur if IBM is at or below $93.00 at expiration. $2.00 - $0.66 = $1.34 loss.

BREAK EVEN

The breakeven point at expiration is the strike price of the short put, minus the premium for which you sold the spread.

In this example, $95.00 - $0.66 = $94.34.

CAPITAL REQUIRED OR BUYING POWER REDUCTION

The amount of buying power necessary to trade a short vertical spread is equal to the position's maximum loss.

For example, if we sold our two strike wide vertical spread for $0.66 ($2.00-$0.66), your capital requirement is $134.00 per spread ($1.34 x 100 shares per contract = $134.00).

VOLATILITY

Because you are both buying and selling options in the same month with the same overall market volatility, the effects of volatility will be somewhat offset by the long and short options.

If implied volatility is high we will be able to sell this credit spread further OTM and still collect our credit of around 1/3 of the width of the strikes, if implied volatility is lower in order to collect our desired credit, we would have to get closer to an ATM strike.

This is a Vega negative trade, so after the play is established, you want implied volatility to decrease.

- If Volatility Increases: Negative Effect
- If Volatility Decreases: Positive Effect

THETA

Passage of Time: Positive

For this type of trade, the net effect of time decay is positive. It will erode the value of the option you sold (good) but it will also erode the value of the option you bought (bad).

ADJUSTMENT

You normally do not adjust this defined risk type of trades, knowing that 33% of these types of trades will be losers, and 66% of the winners.

There are two adjustments that you can make that require no additional capital.

1. You could do a short call spread in the same stock and the same expiration month, in order to collect some additional credit to offset the losses that you are experiencing. If you do decide to go this route, we recommend that you do your short call spread at around the 20 delta for your short strike. The amount of credit that you will receive will depend on how many days there are left to expiration and the implied volatility at the time of your trade. Expect that the additional credit received will be much less than the original credit that you got when you put on the trade.

2. You could "roll" the trade to the next calendar month, by purchasing or closing the current credit spread and simultaneously selling the next month spread. You can do the same strikes that you currently have, or move one or two strikes down, in order to get additional breathing space, but make sure that you do this roll for a net credit. You do not want to pay up for position rolls.

TRADE SUMMARY

Name:	**Short Put Vertical**
Assumption:	Bullish Trade (Positive Delta)
Type:	Credit Spread
Max Profit:	Max Profit Is the Total Credit Received
Max Loss:	Spread Width - Credit Received
Tips:	Sell 30% OTM probability of Expiring
	Collect a min. of 1/3 of Width of the Strikes
	Sell 20 to 60 days before expiry
	One Wide or 2 Wide are the most common.
	Dollar Wide, Penny Wide preferable
Break Even:	Strike Price of the Short Putt (-) Premium Received

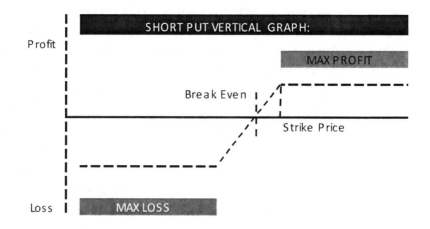

EXITS

It is very, very hard to offer specific rules that you most following to exiting your trades.

There is, however, a perfect number at expiration where you make the most money and achieve max gain. That number is generally the short strike of your trade.

There is also a number where you lose a ton of money or suffer your max loss. If you use the right strategy, you should be closer to the win than the loss. That number is generally the long strike of your trade.

If you use a strategic approach to trading, you have to be willing to lose more, in order to make less. This is the tradeoff of successful trading.

Also, in deciding when to put on a trade you need to pick a "price" both on the winning side and the losing side, so you can recognize if you were right or wrong in your directional assumption.

Over the life of your trade, there is almost a 100% chance of being tested on both sides of the price ranges. It is almost also certain that at some point during the life of the trade you might have a chance to take a profit, and also a chance to take a small loss.

The good trader understands where he stands on the trade between the max win and the max loss, and makes decisions based on that.

Traders rarely take the max win or the max loss, so your ability to manage those profits or losses will determine your success as a trader.

If you have a winning trade you have 3 OPTIONS:
1. Take your profits.
2. Make an addition or adjustment to enhance that position (e.g. making a vertical into a butterfly).
3. Let it go and see if you get to the max profit.

But when you make these choices, you know there is a good chance that the other side could be tested also.

You need to be consistent in your decisions, and only then will you make money on a regular basis.

So when your stock goes to the side of the trade where you are tested both at a profit or a loss, you must make consistent decisions, in order to be successful and make money. That is why as a trader, when you get to your price target you must make a decision, and take action.

On losing trades, Tom likes to let them go to the end, because he likes to give them time and hope the cyclical nature of the market brings back the stock to his desired range.

All this information will make much more sense as you develop as an experienced trader. We will talk a lot more about exits later.

I urge you to reexamine the exit sections of my books periodically during your development as a trader. The more you trade, the more they will make sense to you.

EXITING VERTICAL SPREADS

I know what you want; you want me to give you some specific basic rules for exiting your trades. So here you go...

Exiting a Long Vertical Spread:
- Consider exiting if approximately 70 to 80 percent of potential profit is achieved.
- Also consider exiting if the price target that you set at the initiation of your trade is hit, even though there is still time left on the trade.

- You can also exit if there is upcoming news or an earnings announcement that may significantly impact the underlying stock price.
- Consider exiting 4 to 10 days before expiration to eliminate further trade and gamma risk.

Exiting a Short Vertical Spread:

Use exactly the same suggestions as offered with the long vertical spread above.

LONG CALENDAR SPREADS

The first foundational spread strategy you learned was the vertical spread. The second and equally important spread, and also the foundation of many other spreads, is the calendar.

Calendars are a powerful strategy because they offer a wide profit range, no margin and defined risk. They are considered monthly income trades.

Tom and Tony do not put on many calendar spreads, as they consider them a little boring, because they do not offer or provide instant gratification. On the other hand, they are ideal for people that are not looking for thrills and want to have a stream of steady income month after month.

Calendar spreads can be divided in two main groups:
- Long Call Calendars
- Long Put Call Calendars.

STRATEGY # 11
LONG CALL CALENDAR

DEFINITION
A long call calendar spread is the simultaneous sale of a near term (front month) call and the purchase of a far term (back month) call, with the same strike price. Ideally, the short term option should experience rapid time decay. The long and short options in a long calendar spread must both be calls or both puts.

DIRECTIONAL ASSUMPTION
This trade is considered a neutral strategy if you select your strike at or near ATM. You can also make this trade a directional trade by choosing a strike further OTM. Tom and Tony do not like to do ITM calendar spreads. If you select a strike that happens to be ITM, it is then important that you change your call calendar to a put calendar, in order for the options selected to be OTM.

BENEFITS
Some of the benefits of calendar spreads are:

- low capital requirements
- low margin

- defined risk
- they provide opportunities to collect premium by rolling short month options forward
- they give wide profit margins when your directional assumption plays out.

Because both options use the same strike prices, intrinsic value is the same for both and is canceled out, because you buy one and sell the other. Also because the intrinsic values of the two options cancel each other out in a calendar spread, their value relies only on time value (theta).

THE MECHANICS
If you are bullish, you do a call calendar OTM. Normally you can select for your short strike the first OTM call or the 30% probability of expiring.

PROBABILITY OF SUCCESS
This type trades have a probability of success of around 30% to 40%, depending on which strike you select, but also have a very low probability of losing your full investment.

Look to sell your short options with at least 20 days to expiration and no longer than 30 days. For your back month options you can choose to buy with 60, 90 or a maximum of 120 days.

TIPS
1. If you are anticipating minimal movement on the stock, construct your calendar spread with at-the-money calls. If you're mildly bullish, use slightly OTM calls. This can give you a lower up-front cost.
2. Compare the prices of doing a one month calendar to a 2 month calendar, and try to select the one with the lowest single monthly price.

For example:
The IBM Oct/Nov $100 call calendar = 1.05
The IBM Oct/Dec $100 call calendar = 1.80
To compare similar values you would divide
$1.80/2 (2 months) = $0.90
You would chose the Oct/Dec because of its lower single month
price of $0.90 vs $1.05.

For your short strike selection you can also pick a strike price that you might think the stock can go to, since maximum profit will be achieved if your stock goes to your strike at expiration.

If you decide to do an ITM calendar, you may face exercise risk in your position. So always try to do choose and OTM strike for your calendar spreads.

TRADE EXAMPLE

IBM is now trading at $97.00, and it is September 23rd today. So you decide to sell the $100.00 October call and buy the December $100.00 strike call, for a net debit of $0.90.

MAXIMUM GAIN

Your maximum profit is realized when the stock settles at the strike price selected at expiration.

In this example, if IBM goes up to a value of $100.00 at expiration, your spread will have its maximum worth, because the front month option will expire worthless and the December option, being ATM will have the highest possible price for any option in that calendar month. You can then sell the December $100 call, to close down the trade and realize your profits.

When establishing one-month calendar spreads, you may wish to consider a "risk one to make two" philosophy. That is, for every net debit of $1 at initiation, you're hoping to receive $2 when closing the position.

EXITING THE TRADE

An option's time value is the highest when it is ATM, so you should always look to exit (or think of exiting) this type of trade once your stock reaches your selected strike even if there is still time left on the trade.

Take a look at your spread 1 or 2 weeks before expiration. Analyze the probability of the stock getting back to your selected strike. If the probability of touching your strike is 15% or less, you may consider closing the trade, in order to avoid a full loss on the trade.

In the case of a one month calendar, there is a chance that your selected strike might be reached or hit very close to the day that you put your calendar on. If you take the spread off at that time, your profit will probably be quite small, so you may have to give the trade a bit more of a chance to widen, so you can make a little more profit.

If you happen to have a two month calendar on, you may choose to roll the front month option to the closest back-month option, in order to collect additional premium and get more duration for your trade.

MAXIMUM LOSS

A long calendar spread is a debit spread, so the maximum loss is the original debit of the trade. This loss is realized when the underlying price is so far away from the long calendar spread's strike price that the long back month has zero value on or before expiration.

In this example, this would occur if IBM is well below or above $100.00 at expiration.

BREAK EVEN

On a long calendar spread, the breakeven points are above and below the spread strike price at which the stock or index can close when the near term option expires, and where the far term option's time value is equal to the amount paid for the spread.

This is hard to quantify, because volatility can and does change, and an estimate of the premium value is based on ever-changing implied volatility. But as long as your calendar stays close to your selected strike you should be ok.

In this example, if IBM is between $99 and $101 at expiration, your calendar should be a small winner or at the worst very small loser. Remember, at the $100 strike at expiration, you will have your maximum profit.

CAPITAL REQUIRED OR BUYING POWER REDUCTION

For a long calendar spread, the capital requirement is the total debit paid for the trade ($0.90), and your capital requirement is $90.00 per spread ($0.90 x 100 shares per contract = $90.00).

VOLATILITY

This is a Vega positive trade, so after the play is established you want implied volatility to rise.

- If Volatility Increases: Positive Effect
- If Volatility Decreases: Negative Effect

TIPS

1. Since this type of trade benefits greatly from an increase in implied volatility, it is best to put them on when volatility is low.
2. Also remember that in rising markets volatility normally contracts, and in down side markets volatility expands, which is why many traders prefer put calendars to call calendars.

THETA

Passage of Time: Positive

For this type of trade, the net effect of time decay is positive. It will erode the value of the front option you sold (good), but it will also erode the value of the option you bought but in a much lesser fashion allowing you to profit from the theta differential.

ADJUSTMENT
You normally do not adjust this defined risk type of trade, knowing that 30% to 40% of these types of trades will be losers, and 60-66% winners.

TRADE SUMMARY

Name:	Call Calendar Spread
Assumption:	Bullish Trade (Positive Delta) if bought above price
Type:	Debit Spread
Max Profit:	is realized if stock settles at Strike Selected.
Max Loss:	Is the Original Debit Paid
Tips:	Sell Front Month 20 to 30 days out
	Buy Long Month 60 to 90 Days out
	Buy 30% Prob of Expiring, or 1st OTM Strike
	Better when VIX is Low / High Vega Trade
Break Even:	Are hard to define due to Volatility

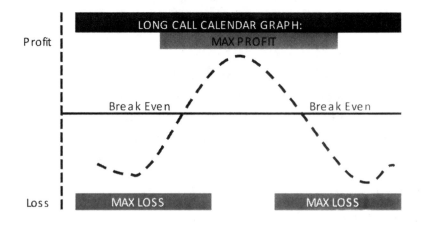

LONG CALL CALENDAR GRAPH:

TRADE # 12
LONG PUT CALENDAR

DEFINITION

A long put calendar spread is the simultaneous sale of a near term (front month) put and the purchase of a far term (back month) put, with the same strike price. Ideally, the short term option should experience rapid time decay. The long and short options in a long calendar spread must both be calls or both puts.

DIRECTIONAL ASSUMPTION

This trade is considered a neutral strategy if you select your strike at or near ATM. You can also make this trade a directional trade, by choosing strike further OTM. Tom and Tony do not like to do ITM calendar spreads, because if you select a strike that happens to be ITM, it is then important you change your put calendar to a call calendar, in order for the options selected to be OTM.

BENEFITS

Some of the benefits of calendar spreads are:

- low capital requirements
- low margin
- defined risk

- they provide opportunities to collect premium by rolling short month options forward
- they provide wide profit margins when your directional assumption plays out.

Because both options use the same strike prices, intrinsic value is the same for both and is canceled out, because you buy one and sell the other. Also, because the intrinsic values of the two options cancel each other out in a calendar spread, their value relies only on time value (theta).

THE MECHANICS
If you are bearish, you do a put calendar OTM. Normally you can select for your short strike the first OTM put or the 30% probability of expiring.

TIPS
1. If you are anticipating minimal movement on the stock, construct your calendar spread with ATM puts.
2. If you're mildly bearish, use slightly OTM puts. This can give you a lower up-front cost.

PROBABILITY OF SUCCESS
This type of trade has a probability of success of around 30% to 40%, depending on which strike you select. But they also have a very low probability of losing your full investment,
Look to sell your short options with at least 20 days to expiration, and no longer than 30 days. For your back month options you can choose to buy with 60, 90 or a maximum of 120 days.

TIP
Compare the prices of doing a one month calendar to a 2 month calendar, and try to select the one with the lowest single monthly price.

For example:
The IBM Oct/Nov $95 put calendar = 1.05
The IBM Oct/Dec $95 put calendar = 1.80
To compare similar values you would divide $1.80/2 (2 months) =$0.90
You would choose the Oct/Dec, because of its lower single month price.

For your short strike selection you can also pick a strike price that you might think the stock can go to, since maximum profit will be achieved if your stock goes to your strike at expiration.

If you decide to do an ITM calendar, you may face exercise risk in your position. So always try to choose an OTM strike for your calendar spreads.

TRADE EXAMPLE

IBM is now trading at $97.00 and it is September 23rd today. So you decide to sell the $95.00 October put and buy the December (2 month Wide) $95.00 strike put for a net debit of $0.90.

MAXIMUM GAIN

Your maximum profit is realized when the stock settles at the strike price selected at expiration.

In this example, if IBM goes down to a value of $95.00 at expiration, your spread will have its maximum worth, because the front month option will expire worthless and the December option being ATM will have the highest possible price for any option in that calendar month. You can then sell the December $95 put to close down the trade and realize your profits.

When establishing one month calendar spreads, you may wish to consider a "risk one to make two" philosophy. That is, for every net debit of $1 at initiation, you're hoping to receive $2 when closing the position.

EXITING THE TRADE

An option's time value is the highest when it is ATM, so you should always look to exit (or think of exiting) this type of trade once your stock reaches your selected strike - even if there is still time left on the trade.

Take a look at your spread one or 2 weeks before expiration. Analyze the probability of the stock getting back to your selected strike. If the probability of touching your strike is 15% or less, you may consider closing the trade, in order to avoid a full loss on the trade.

In the case of a one month calendar, there is a chance that your selected strike might be reached or hit very close to the day that you put your calendar on. If you take the spread off at that time your profit will probably be quite small, so you may have to give the trade a bit more of a chance to widen, so you can make a little more profit.

If you happen to have a two month calendar on, you may choose to roll the front month option to the closest back month option, in order to collect additional premium and get more duration for your trade.

MAXIMUM LOSS

A long calendar spread is a debit spread, so the maximum loss is the original debit of the trade. This loss is realized when the underlying price is so far away from the long calendar spread's strike price that the long back month has zero value on or before expiration.

In our example, this would happen if IBM is well below or above $95.00 at expiration.

BREAK EVEN

On a long calendar spread, the breakeven points are above and below the spread strike price at which the stock or index can close when the near term option expires, and where the far term option's time value is equal to the amount paid for the spread.

This is hard to quantify, because volatility can and does change, and an estimate of the premium value is based on ever changing implied volatility. But as long as your calendar stays closer to your selected strike, you should be ok.

In our example, if IBM is between $94 and $96 at expiration, your calendar should be a small winner or at the worst very small loser. Remember, at the $95 strike at expiration you will have your maximum profit.

CAPITAL REQUIRED OR BUYING POWER REDUCTION

For a long calendar spread, the capital requirement is the total debit paid for the trade ($0.90), and your capital requirement is $90.00 per spread ($0.90 x 100 shares per contract = $90.00).

VOLATILITY

This is a Vega positive trade, so after the play is established, you want implied volatility to rise.

- If Volatility Increases: Positive Effect
- If Volatility Decreases: Negative Effect

TIPS

1. Since this type of trade benefits greatly from an increase in implied volatility, it is best to put them on when volatility is low.
2. Also remember that in rising markets, volatility normally contracts and in down side markets volatility expands, which is why many traders prefer put calendars to call calendars.

THETA

Passage of Time: Positive

For this type of trade, the net effect of time decay is positive. It will erode the value of the front option you sold (good), but it will also erode the value of the option you bought but in a much lesser fashion, allowing you to profit from the theta differential.

ADJUSTMENT

You normally do not adjust this defined risk type of trades, knowing that 30% to 40% of these types of trades will be losers, and 60-66% of the winners.

TRADE SUMMARY

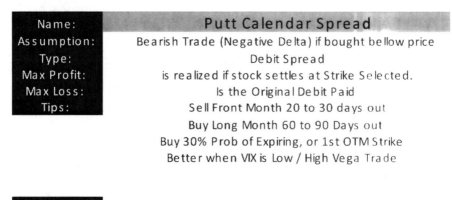

Name:	Putt Calendar Spread
Assumption:	Bearish Trade (Negative Delta) if bought bellow price
Type:	Debit Spread
Max Profit:	is realized if stock settles at Strike Selected.
Max Loss:	Is the Original Debit Paid
Tips:	Sell Front Month 20 to 30 days out
	Buy Long Month 60 to 90 Days out
	Buy 30% Prob of Expiring, or 1st OTM Strike
	Better when VIX is Low / High Vega Trade

Break Even:	Are hard to define due to Volatility

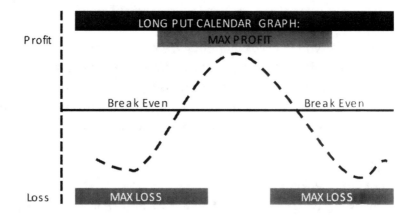

STRATEGY # 13
IRON CONDOR

DEFINITION

The iron condor is a very popular spread that combines short call and short put verticals. Typically, the stock price will be between your short call strike and your short put strike when you construct your spread. If the stock is not in the center at initiation, the strategy will be either bullish or bearish.

The width between your short and long call strikes and your short and long put strikes are usually the same. However, the distance between both of your short strikes may vary, to give you a wider area from where to profit.

DIRECTIONAL ASSUMPTION

An iron condor is a market neutral, defined risk position that profits from positive time decay (theta). It can be profitable over a wide range of stock prices at expiration, giving you a large sweet spot from where to achieve your maximum profit.

If the current stock price is not in the center of the iron condor (between both short strikes) at the initiation of the trade, the strategy will be either bullish or bearish.

You do this trade if you're anticipating minimal movement on the stock within a specific time frame.

THE MECHANICS
1. You construct this trade buy selling an OTM Put Vertical, and an OTM Short Call vertical spread.
2. Iron Condors are normally done with the vertical spread being one or two strikes wide.
3. You may wish to consider ensuring that both your short strikes are around one standard deviation or more away from the stock price at initiation. That will increase your probability of success. However, the further these strike prices are from the current stock price, the lower the potential profit will be from this strategy.
4. Normally you want to collect at least 30% of the width of the strikes. That can sometimes be accomplished by selling the 30% probability of expiring strike or somewhere around that area.

TIPS
1. Tom & Tony like to do more aggressive trades. On Iron Condors they try to collect 40 to 50% of the width of the strikes. Those parameters give the trade a smaller probability of success, but collect a higher credit.
2. Look for options with at least 20 days to expiration and no longer than 60 days.
3. If you are in a sideways trending market, this strategy can become a consistent way to make money, month in and out.

TRADE EXAMPLE
IBM is now trading at $100.00 and you decide to sell the $95.00 / $93.00 short put vertical, and the $105.00 / $107.00 short call vertical for a net credit of $0.70.

TIP
It's generally most efficient to execute iron condors as a single trade. Attempting to leg into the position via four individual calls and puts, or via call and put vertical spreads can expose you to significant execution

risk. The likelihood of option premium movement for one leg before the entire position is established is very high. This may result in a poor overall credit for the iron condor, subpar profit potential and increased overall risk.

MAXIMUM GAIN
Profit is limited to the net credit received. This happens if your stock is between both short strikes you selected.

In our IBM example, maximum profit would occur if the stock closes between $95.00 and $105.00 at expiration.

EXITING THE TRADE
Exiting an iron condor is a function of both time and price. You may consider exiting the trade at any time you have achieved a profit of 50% of more. Tom and Tony rarely adjust iron condors. If your trade was placed fundamentally correctly, allow the trade time to go your way and generate a profit.

MAXIMUM LOSS
The maximum loss is the dollar value (width) of the difference between the two strike prices of either the short call vertical spread or the short put vertical spread (whichever is greater) minus the credit. Maximum loss occurs if the underlying stock's price is below the long put's strike price or above the long call's strike price at expiration.

BREAK EVEN
There are two break-even points:
- On the Put side, Short put strike minus the net credit received.
- On the call side, Short call strike plus the net credit received.

In our IBM example, the break even points are:
$95.00 (-) $0.70 = $94.30 on the put side.
$105.00 (+) $0.70 = $105.70 on the call side.

CAPITAL REQUIRED OR BUYING POWER REDUCTION

The buying power necessary to trade an iron condor is equal to the maximum loss on the entire position. This is not the total risk of both the short call vertical and short put vertical spreads, because only one can lose at expiration.

In our example, the Max loss is equal to $2.00 (-) $0.70 = $1.30 of risk per spread.

VOLATILITY

This is a Vega negative trade, so after the play is established, you want implied volatility to fall.

- If Volatility Increases: Positive Effect
- If Volatility Decreases: Negative Effect

TIP

The higher the implied volatility when you put on your trade, the wider you can make your short strikes.

THETA

Passage of Time: Positive

For this type of trade, the net effect of time decay is positive. You want all four legs to expire worthless.

TRADE SUMMARY

Name:	**Short Iron Condor**
Assumption:	Neutral Strategy
Type:	Credit Spread
Max Profit:	Credit Received
Max Loss:	Spread Width - Credit Received
Tips:	Sell Both Calls and Putts with 30% prob of Expiring or 1 TSD
	Collect at least 30% of Spread width
	Sell 20 to 40 Days out

Break Even:	Are the Sold Strikes plus and Minus the Credit received

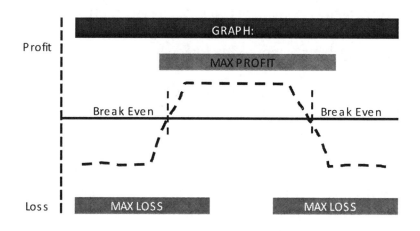

STRATEGY # 14
BUTTERFLY

DEFINITION
A butterfly spread is a combination of a long and short vertical spread. This is a low risk, high reward strategy with a low probability of success. Butterfly spreads make most of their money near expiration day.

DIRECTIONAL ASSUMPTION
This trade could be both a neutral trade if done with ATM strikes, or it could also be bullish or bearish if you do OTM calls or OTM puts respectively.

It's important to sell the strike price at which you believe the stock or index is going to close at expiration. If you expect the stock to head sideways, sell ATM options. Remember, selling ATM produces the greatest potential to benefit from theta decay.

THE MECHANICS
A long butterfly spread is a combination of a long vertical spread and a short vertical spread, with both spreads having the same short strike.

PROBABILITY OF SUCCESS
It is a low probability, high reward strategy. The probability of success of a butterfly is equal to approximately the debit paid divided by the width of the short strike and the long strike.

For example, if you pay $0.20 cents for the $98/$100/$102 IBM call calendar, this trade will have an approximately 10% probability of success: 0.20/2.00 = 0.1 x100 = 10% probability of success.

Ideally, you want the short options to expire worthless, by having the stock end up at expiration right at your short strike.

TIPS

1. The key to the butterfly is that the width between the 3 strikes is the same.
2. Some investors may wish to run this play using index options rather than options on individual stocks. That's because historically, indices have not been as volatile as individual stocks. Fluctuations in an index's component stock prices tend to cancel one another out lessening the volatility of the index as a whole.
3. Since this is a low probability trade, the amount of capital you assign to this type of strategy should be much less than your regular lot or trade size.
4. Because butterflies widen much more on expiration week, you can put on this type of trade closer to expiration, thus having a bit more certainty about where the stock could end up at expiration.

TRADE EXAMPLE
IBM now trading at $97.00.

OTM Call Butterfly Example:
(Slightly bullish trade) – 2 strikes wide
Buy 1 $98 call
Sell 2 $100 calls
Buy 1 $102 calls for a net debit of $0.20 cents.

OTM Put Butterfly Example:
(Slightly Bearish trade) -1 Strike wide

Buy 1 $98 puts
Sell 2 $97 puts
Buy 1 $96 puts for a net debit of $0.10 cents.

MAXIMUM GAIN

Potential profit is limited to any of the long strikes minus the short strike, minus the net debit paid. If the stock finishes anywhere between your long strikes, you will make money.

For example in the IBM Call Butterfly:
$102.00 - $100.00 = $2.000 minus 0.20 = 1.80

EXITING THE TRADE

Tom and Tony like to exit butterfly spreads when they can sell for double what they paid.

MAXIMUM LOSS

Risk is limited to the net debit paid originally for the trade.

Break Even

There are two breakeven points on a butterfly spread. If the stock closes between the two breakeven points, you make money.
1. First, simply subtract the net debit from the higher purchased strike price, to calculate the upper breakeven point.
2. Then, add your net debit to the lower purchased strike price to find the lower breakeven point, not including commissions.

CAPITAL REQUIRED OR BUYING POWER REDUCTION

For a long butterfly spread, the buying power reduction is equal to the net debit paid.

VOLATILITY

This is a Vega negative trade, so after the play is established, you want implied volatility to fall.

- If Volatility Increases: Negative Effect
- If Volatility Decreases: Positive Effect

TIP

Butterflies are cheapest when volatility is high, because it is much harder to predict the final price of a stock on expiration when implied volatility is high, due to rapid price movement on the underlying.

THETA

Passage of Time: Positive

For this type of trade, the net effect of time decay is positive. Ideally, you want your short options to expire worthless.

TRADE SUMMARY

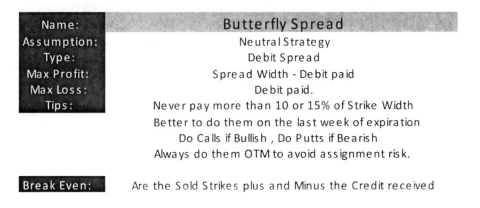

Name:	Butterfly Spread
Assumption:	Neutral Strategy
Type:	Debit Spread
Max Profit:	Spread Width - Debit paid
Max Loss:	Debit paid.
Tips:	Never pay more than 10 or 15% of Strike Width
	Better to do them on the last week of expiration
	Do Calls if Bullish , Do Putts if Bearish
	Always do them OTM to avoid assignment risk.
Break Even:	Are the Sold Strikes plus and Minus the Credit received

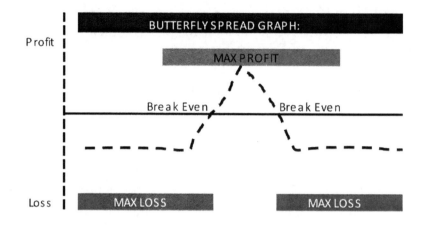

DIAGONAL SPREADS

There are two types of diagonal spreads; in the money (ITM) and out of the money (OTM). It's important to understand how to trade both, because they take advantage of different situations.

Diagonals are a combination of verticals and calendar spreads. They allow more direction, while still taking advantage of positive time decay and a rise in implied volatility

Diagonal spreads can be divided in two main groups:
- ITM Diagonal Spreads
- OTM Diagonal Spreads.

ITM Diagonal Spreads can also be divided into two groups:
- ITM call diagonals (aka leveraged covered calls or calendarized long call verticals).
- ITM put diagonals (aka leveraged covered puts or calendarized long put verticals).

OTM Diagonal Spreads can also divide into two groups:
- OTM call diagonals (aka calendarized short call verticals).
- OTM put diagonals (aka calendarized short put verticals.

STRATEGY #15
ITM CALL DIAGONAL
(aka CALENDARIZED LONG CALL VERTICAL or LEVERAGED COVERED CALL)

DEFINITION

A long call (bullish) ITM diagonal spread is constructed by buying a back month ITM call option and selling a front month OTM call option at the same time. Both expirations and strikes are different. Typically, an investor buys one or two ITM strikes and sells one or two OTM strikes.

This strategy is often referred as a leveraged covered call, because you substitute your long stock position with a long dated ITM call, thus requiring much less capital to put on the trade than a traditional covered call.

DIRECTIONAL ASSUMPTION

An ITM call diagonal spread is a bullish trade, and similar to a calendar spread, with the main difference being their strike prices. A diagonal spread allows you to trade with more of a directional bias than a calendar spread, while still benefiting from an ability to roll out the spread, take advantage of time decay and profit from changes in implied volatility.

Of course, there are additional risks to keep in mind as well: Long ITM calls, unlike stock, eventually expire, and when they do, it's possible that you could lose the entire value of your initial investment.

Unlike a covered call (where you typically wouldn't mind being assigned on the short option), when running an ITM call diagonal you don't want to be assigned on the short call, because you don't actually own the stock yet. You only own the right to buy the stock at your long call price.

THE MECHANICS

1. The first step is to select a long dated ITM call that will see price changes similar to the stock.
2. So look for a call with a delta of .70 or .80 or even higher. As a starting point, when searching for an appropriate delta, check options that are at least 20% ITM. But for a particularly volatile stock, you may need to go deeper ITM to find the delta you're looking for.
3. Look to sell your short options with at least 20 days to expiration and no longer than 30 days. For your back month options, you can choose to buy with 60, 90 or a maximum of 120 days.
4. You can sell your front month option at a 30% probability of expiring or the first OTM option. The further out you sell your short call, the more directional your play will be. For your short strike selection you can also pick a strike price that you might think the stock can go to, since maximum profit will be achieved if your stock goes to your strike at expiration.

TIPS

1. Some investors choose to run this strategy on expensive stocks that they would like to trade, but don't want to spend the capital to buy at least 100 shares.

2. It is generally more efficient to enter ITM diagonal spreads as a single trade. If you enter in one leg at a time, the higher deltas of the spread's individual legs may cause the price of the individual option premiums to move against you before you can establish the entire position.

TRADE EXAMPLE
IBM is now trading at $95.00 and it is September 23rd today, so you decide to sell the $100.00 October Call and buy the December (2 month Wide) $90.00 strike put for a net debit of $5.50.

MAXIMUM GAIN
Your maximum profit on a diagonal spread is the width between the long strike and short strike, minus the debit. That said, a popular way to trade this strategy is to treat it like a covered call.

You want the stock to remain as close to the strike price of the short option as possible on expiration, without going above it.

Potential profit is limited to the premium received for sale of the front-month call plus the performance of the ITM call.

EXITING THE TRADE
For exiting this type of trade you have two options, rolling the front month short call, or closing down the entire position completely.

Consider rolling the short option:
- Four to five days before expiration.
- When the short option is 10% of the value of the strike price width.
- When the stock is trading at your short strike price.
- Anytime you want to buy it back, to allow your long option to make money.

TIPS

1. If the stock price exceeds the strike price of the short option before expiration, you might want to consider closing out the entire position. If the strategy was implemented correctly, you could even see a profit in such a case.
2. If you do get assigned on the short call, don't make the mistake of exercising the long ITM call. Sell the ITM call, so you'll capture the time value (if there's any remaining) along with the intrinsic value. Simultaneously buy the stock, to cover your newly credited short stock position.

MAXIMUM LOSS

An ITM diagonal spread is a debit spread, so your maximum loss is the debit paid.

BREAK EVEN

An ITM diagonal's breakeven point is the long strike plus the net debit. This breakeven point does not take into consideration any rolls that may occur.

CAPITAL REQUIRED OR BUYING POWER REDUCTION

For a long diagonal spread, the capital requirement is the total debit paid for the trade.

VOLATILITY

After the trade is established, the effect of implied volatility is somewhat neutral. Although it will increase the value of the call you sold (bad), it will also increase the value of the ITM call you bought (good).

THETA

Passage of Time: Positive

For this type of trade, time decay is your friend, because the front-month option(s) you sell will lose their value faster than the back-month long ITM call.

TRADE SUMMARY

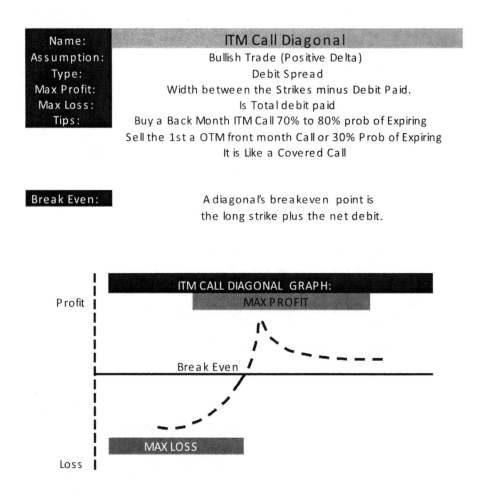

Name:	ITM Call Diagonal
Assumption:	Bullish Trade (Positive Delta)
Type:	Debit Spread
Max Profit:	Width between the Strikes minus Debit Paid.
Max Loss:	Is Total debit paid
Tips:	Buy a Back Month ITM Call 70% to 80% prob of Expiring
	Sell the 1st a OTM front month Call or 30% Prob of Expiring
	It is Like a Covered Call

Break Even:	A diagonal's breakeven point is the long strike plus the net debit.

ITM CALL DIAGONAL GRAPH:

MAX PROFIT

Profit

Break Even

MAX LOSS

Loss

STRATEGY # 16
ITM PUT DIAGONAL
(aka CALENDARIZED LONG
PUT VERTICAL
or LEVERAGED COVERED PUT)

DEFINITION

A long put (bearish) ITM diagonal spread is constructed by buying a back month ITM put option and selling a front month OTM put option at the same time. Both expirations and strikes are different. Typically, an investor buys one or two ITM strikes and sells one or two OTM strikes.

This strategy is often referred as a leveraged covered put, because you substitute your short stock position with a long dated ITM put, thus requiring much less capital to put on the trade than a traditional covered put.

DIRECTIONAL ASSUMPTION

An ITM put diagonal spread is a bearish trade, and similar to a calendar spread, with the main difference being their strike prices. A diagonal spread allows you to trade with more of a directional bias than a calendar spread, while still benefiting from an ability to roll out the spread, take advantage of time decay and profit from changes in implied volatility.

Of course, there are additional risks to keep in mind as well. Long ITM puts, unlike stock, eventually expire, and when they do, it's possible that you could lose the entire value of your initial investment.

Unlike a covered put (where you typically wouldn't mind being assigned on the short option), when running an ITM put diagonal you don't want to be assigned on the short put, because you are not short the stock yet. You only own the right to sell the stock at your long put price.

THE MECHANICS

1. The first step is to select a long dated ITM put that will see price changes similar to the stock. So look for a put with a delta of .70 or .80 or even higher.

2. As a starting point, when searching for an appropriate delta, check options that are at least 20% ITM. But for a particularly volatile stock, you may need to go deeper ITM to find the delta you're looking for.

3. Look to sell your short options with at least 20 days to expiration and no longer than 30 days. For your back month options you can choose to buy with 60, 90 or a maximum of 120 days.

4. You can sell your front month option at a 30% probability of expiring or the first OTM option. The further out you sell your short put, the more directional your play will be. For your short strike selection you can also pick a strike price that you might think the stock can go to, since maximum profit will be achieved if your stock goes to your strike at expiration.

TIPS

1. Some investors choose to run this strategy on expensive stocks that they would like to trade, but don't want to spend the capital to sell at least 100 shares.

2. It is generally more efficient to enter ITM diagonal spreads as a single trade. If you enter in one leg at a time, the higher deltas of the spread's individual legs may cause the price of the individual option premiums to move against you before you can establish the entire position.

TRADE EXAMPLE

IBM is now trading at $95.00 and it is September 23rd today. So you decide to sell the $90.00 October put and buy the December (2 month Wide) $100.00 strike put for a net debit of $5.50.

MAXIMUM GAIN

Your maximum profit on a diagonal spread is the width between the long strike and short strike minus the debit. That said, a popular way to trade this strategy is to treat it like a covered put.

You want the stock to remain as close to the strike price of the short option as possible on expiration, without going below it.

Potential profit is limited to the premium received for sale of the front-month put, plus the performance of the ITM put.

EXITING THE TRADE

For exiting this type of trade you have two options, rolling the front month short put, or closing down the entire position completely.

Consider rolling the short option:
- Four to five days before expiration.
- When the short option is 10% of the value of the strike price width.
- When the stock is trading at your short strike price.
- Anytime you want to buy it back to allow your long option to make money.

TIPS

1. If the stock price falls past the strike price of the short option before expiration, you might want to consider closing out the entire position. If the strategy was implemented correctly, you could even see a profit in such a case.
2. If you do get assigned on the short put, don't make the mistake of exercising the long ITM put. Sell the ITM put, so you'll capture the time value (if there's any remaining) along with the intrinsic value. Simultaneously sell the stock, to cover your newly credited long stock position.

MAXIMUM LOSS

An ITM diagonal spread is a debit spread, so your maximum loss is the debit paid.

BREAK EVEN

An ITM diagonal's breakeven point is the long strike plus the net debit. This breakeven point does not take into consideration any rolls that may occur.

CAPITAL REQUIRED OR BUYING POWER REDUCTION

For a long diagonal spread, the capital requirement is the total debit paid for the trade.

VOLATILITY

After the trade is established, the effect of implied volatility is somewhat neutral. Although it will increase the value of the put you sold (bad), it will also increase the value of the ITM put you bought (good).

THETA

Passage of Time: Positive

For this type of trade, time decay is your friend, because the front-month option(s) you sell will lose their value faster than the back-month long ITM put.

TRADE SUMMARY

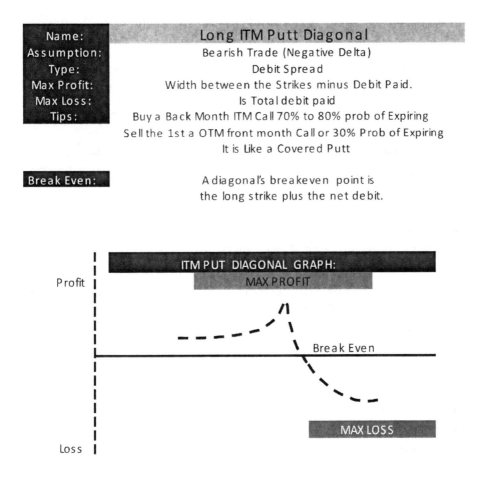

Name:	Long ITM Putt Diagonal
Assumption:	Bearish Trade (Negative Delta)
Type:	Debit Spread
Max Profit:	Width between the Strikes minus Debit Paid.
Max Loss:	Is Total debit paid
Tips:	Buy a Back Month ITM Call 70% to 80% prob of Expiring
	Sell the 1st a OTM front month Call or 30% Prob of Expiring
	It is Like a Covered Putt
Break Even:	A diagonal's breakeven point is the long strike plus the net debit.

ITM PUT DIAGONAL GRAPH:

Profit

MAX PROFIT

Break Even

MAX LOSS

Loss

STRATEGY # 17
OTM CALL DIAGONAL
(aka CALENDARIZED
SHORT CALL VERTICAL)

DEFINITION

An OTM diagonal spread is a combination of a short vertical and a calendar spread. An OTM call is constructed by selling an OTM call, (approximately 30 days from expiration – "front-month"), and the purchasing of a further OTM call, approximately 60 to 90 days from expiration – "back-month"). Generally, the stock will be below the short front month call.

You can think of this as a two-step play. It's a cross between a long calendar spread with calls and a short call spread. It starts out as a time decay play. Then once you roll your front month call to a second call with the same expiration as the back month call you originally purchased, (after front-month expiration), you have legged into a short call spread. Ideally, after the roll you will be able to establish this play for a net credit or for a small net debit. Then, the sale of the second call will be all gravy.

The concept behind the OTM diagonal spread's structure is to bring the cost basis down on a calendar spread, by adding a short vertical spread to it.

DIRECTIONAL ASSUMPTION

An OTM diagonal is not as directional in nature as an ITM diagonal. For an OTM diagonal spread, it is desirable for the underlying stock to remain relatively stable. This trade is like a calendar spread, because its profit potential lies in taking advantage of time decay in combination with the ability to roll forward.

TIP

You can do the spread 1 or 2 strikes wide.

THE MECHANICS

1. Sell a front month call, at either 30% Probability of Expiring or the 1st OTM Call and buy a back month higher call with 60 to 90 days to expiration.
2. Look to sell your short options with at least 20 days to expiration and no longer than 30 days. For your back month options you can choose to buy with 60, 90 or a maximum of 120 days.
3. For your short strike selection you can also pick a strike price that you might think the stock can go to since maximum profit will be achieved if your stock goes to your strike at expiration.
4. Open interest should be a minimum of 20 times the number of contracts traded. Look for tight bid/ask spreads or penny wide markets.
5. Evaluate implied volatility (best if it is relatively low).
6. This is normally a debit spread.

TRADE EXAMPLE

IBM is now trading at $102.00, and it is September 23rd today, so you decide to sell the $105.00 October call and buy the December (2 month Wide) $110.00 strike call for a net debit of $1.90.

MAXIMUM GAIN

Much like the calendar spread, maximum gain is realized if the underlying stock is trading at your short strike price at expiration.

If IBM goes up to a value of $105.00 at expiration, you have two choices:

1. *Roll the October call that you are short to a November call, if you can roll for a credit similar to the debit paid. You will have reduced your risk to only the difference between the spread strikes.*
2. *Another alternative is to close down the trade and take your profits.*

For every the month where you have a front month short option, you want the stock price to stay at or around your short strike until expiration of the front-month option. When you rolled to month when you purchased your long option, in that moment you turned your diagonal into a vertical, and then you'll want the stock price to be below your short strike when the back-month option expires.

Rolling your short call:
Consider rolling an OTM diagonal spread

- Four to five days before expiration.
- When the short option is 10 percent of the value of the strike price width.
- When the stock is trading at your short strike price.

After front-month expiration, you have legged into a short call vertical spread. So the effect of implied volatility depends on where the stock is, relative to your strike prices.

If your assumption was correct and the stock price is approaching or below your short strike, you want implied volatility to decrease. That's because it will decrease the value of both options, and ideally you want them to expire worthless.

If your assumption was incorrect and the stock price is approaching or above your short strike, you want implied volatility to increase for two reasons. First, it will increase the value of the near-the-money option you bought faster than the ITM option you sold, thereby decreasing the overall value of the spread. Second, it reflects an increased probability of a price swing (which will hopefully be to the downside).

MAXIMUM LOSS

The maximum loss is the difference between the long and short strike, minus the credit received or plus the debit paid.

In our example this would happen if IBM is well below or above $105.00 at expiration.

BREAK EVEN

It is possible to approximate break-even points, but there are too many variables to give an exact formula.

On a diagonal spread, the breakeven points are above and below the spread's strike price at which the stock can close when the near term option expires, and where the far term option's time value is equal to the amount paid for the spread.

This again is difficult to quantify, because implied volatility can and does change, and an estimate of the premium value is based on ever changing implied volatility.

CAPITAL REQUIRED OR BUYING POWER REDUCTION

For an OTM diagonal spread, the capital requirement is the difference between long and short strikes, minus credit received or plus debit paid.

VOLATILITY

This is a Vega positive trade, so after the play is established, you want implied volatility to rise.

- If Volatility Increases: Positive Effect
- If Volatility Decreases: Negative Effect

TIP

Since this type of trade benefits greatly from an increase in implied volatility it is best to put them on when volatility is low.

You're better off if implied volatility increases close to front-month expiration. That way you will receive a higher premium when rolling or closing your trade.

THETA

Passage of Time: Positive

For this type of trade, the net effect of time decay is positive. It will erode the value of the front option you sold (good), but it will also erode the value of the option you bought but in a much lesser fashion allowing you to profit from the theta differential.

ADJUSTMENT

There is no adjustment for this type of trade. When you do a roll to a following month for a net credit, your original risk will be reduced by the amount of the credit received.

TRADE SUMMARY

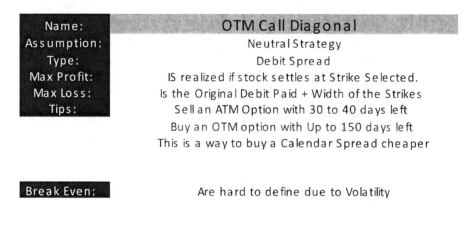

Name:	OTM Call Diagonal
Assumption:	Neutral Strategy
Type:	Debit Spread
Max Profit:	IS realized if stock settles at Strike Selected.
Max Loss:	Is the Original Debit Paid + Width of the Strikes
Tips:	Sell an ATM Option with 30 to 40 days left
	Buy an OTM option with Up to 150 days left
	This is a way to buy a Calendar Spread cheaper
Break Even:	Are hard to define due to Volatility

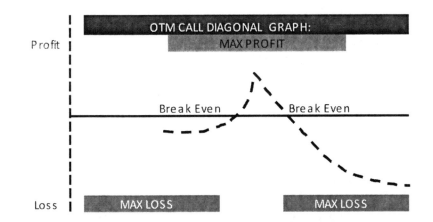

STRATEGY # 18
OTM PUT DIAGONAL
(aka CALENDARIZED
SHORT PUT VERTICAL)

DEFINITION

An OTM diagonal spread is a combination of a short vertical and a calendar spread. An OTM put diagonal is constructed by selling an OTM put, (approximately 30 days from expiration – "front-month"), and purchasing a further OTM put, approximately 60 to 90 days from expiration – "back-month"). Generally, the stock will be below the short front month call.

You can think of this as a two-step play. It's a cross between a long calendar spread with puts and a short put spread. It starts out as a time decay play. Then once you roll your front month put to a second put with the same expiration as the back month put you originally purchased, (after front-month expiration), you have legged into a short put spread. Ideally, you will be able to establish this play for a net credit or for a small net debit. Then, the sale of the second put will be all gravy.

The concept behind the OTM diagonal spread's structure is to bring the cost basis down on a calendar spread, by adding a short vertical spread to it.

DIRECTIONAL ASSUMPTION

An OTM diagonal is not as directional in nature as an ITM diagonal. For an OTM diagonal spread, it is desirable for the underlying stock to remain relatively stable. This trade is like a calendar spread, because its profit potential lies in taking advantage of time decay in combination with the ability to roll forward.

TIP

You can do the spread 1 or 2 strikes wide.

THE MECHANICS

1. Sell a front month put, at either 30% probability of expiring or the 1st OTM put, and buy a back month put with 60 to 90 days to expiration.
2. Look to sell your short options with at least 20 days to expiration and no longer than 30 days. For your back month options you can choose to buy with 60, 90 or a maximum of 120 days.
3. For your short strike selection you can also pick a strike price that you might think the stock can go to, since maximum profit will be achieved if your stock goes to your strike at expiration.
4. Open interest should be a minimum of 20 times the number of contracts traded. Look for tight bid/ask spreads or penny wide markets.
5. Evaluate implied volatility (best if it is relatively low).
6. This is normally a debit spread.

TRADE EXAMPLE

IBM is now trading at $98.00 and it is September 23rd today, so you decide to sell the $95.00 October put and buy the December (2 month Wide) $90.00 strike put for a net debit of $1.90.

MAXIMUM GAIN

Much like the calendar spread, maximum gain is realized if the underlying stock is trading at your short strike price at expiration.

If IBM goes down to a value of $95.00 at expiration, you have two choices:

1. *Roll the October put that you are short to a November put, if you can roll for a credit similar to the debit paid. You will have reduced your risk to only the difference between the spread strikes.*
2. *Another alternative is to close down the trade and taking your profits.*

For every the month where you have a front month short option, you want the stock price to stay at or around your short strike until expiration of the front-month option. When you rolled to month when you purchased your long option, in that moment you turned your diagonal into a vertical, and then you'll want the stock price to be below your short strike when the back-month option expires.

Rolling your short put:
- Consider rolling an OTM diagonal spread,
- Four to five days before expiration.
- When the short option is 10 percent of the value of the strike price width.
- When the stock is trading at your short strike price.

After front-month expiration, you have legged into a short put vertical spread. So the effect of implied volatility depends on where the stock is relative to your strike prices.

If your assumption was correct and the stock price is approaching or above your short strike, you want implied volatility to decrease. That's because it will decrease the value of both options, and ideally you want them to expire worthless.

If your assumption was incorrect and the stock price is approaching or below your short strike, you want implied volatility to increase for two reasons. First, it will increase the value of the near-the-money option you bought faster than the ITM option you sold, thereby decreasing the overall value of the spread. Second, it reflects an increased probability of a price swing (which will hopefully be to the downside).

MAXIMUM LOSS

The maximum loss is the difference between the long and short strike, minus the credit received or plus the debit paid.

In our example, this would happen if IBM is well below or above $95.00 at expiration.

BREAK EVEN

It is possible to approximate break-even points, but there are too many variables to give an exact formula.

On a diagonal spread, the breakeven points are above and below the spread's strike price at which the stock can close when the near term option expires, and where the far term option's time value is equal to the amount paid for the spread.

This again is difficult to quantify, because implied volatility can and does change, and an estimate of the premium value is based on ever changing implied volatility.

CAPITAL REQUIRED OR BUYING POWER REDUCTION

For an OTM diagonal spread, the capital requirement is the difference between long and short strikes, minus credit received or plus debit paid.

VOLATILITY

This is a Vega positive trade, so after the play is established, you want implied volatility to rise.

- If Volatility Increases: Positive Effect
- If Volatility Decreases: Negative Effect

TIP

Since this type of trade's benefits greatly from an increase in implied volatility, it is best to put them on when volatility is low.

You're better off if implied volatility increases close to front-month expiration. That way you will receive a higher premium when rolling or closing your trade.

THETA

Passage of Time: Positive

For this type of trade, the net effect of time decay is positive. It will erode the value of the front option you sold (good), but it will also erode the value of the option you bought but in a much lesser fashion allowing you to profit from the theta differential.

ADJUSTMENT

There is no adjustment for this type of trade. When you do a roll to a following month for a net credit, your original risk will be reduced by the amount of the credit received.

TRADE SUMMARY

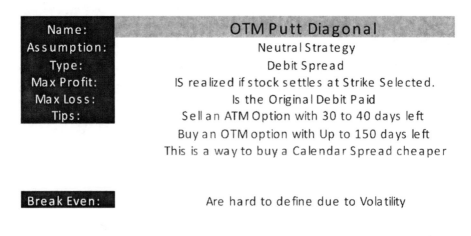

Name:	OTM Putt Diagonal
Assumption:	Neutral Strategy
Type:	Debit Spread
Max Profit:	IS realized if stock settles at Strike Selected.
Max Loss:	Is the Original Debit Paid
Tips:	Sell an ATM Option with 30 to 40 days left
	Buy an OTM option with Up to 150 days left
	This is a way to buy a Calendar Spread cheaper
Break Even:	Are hard to define due to Volatility

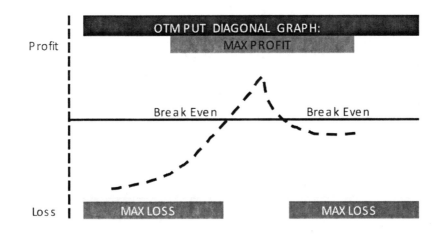

STRATEGY # 19
SHORT STRADDLE

DEFINITION

A short straddle is the simultaneous sale of an ATM call and an ATM put.

A **long straddle**, on the other hand, is exactly the opposite, it is buying an ATM call and ATM put. Tom and Tony never buy a long straddle, because they have a very small probability of success and they are also theta negative. In order to make money on a long straddle you need an almost immediate very large move. So for this reason, we can forget about the long straddle and focus on one of the best trading strategies - the short straddle.

DIRECTIONAL ASSUMPTION

A short straddle trade is considered a neutral strategy; you're expecting minimal movement on the stock. In fact, you want to be darned certain that the stock will stick close to the ATM strike.

A short straddle gives you the obligation to sell the stock at the ATM strike sold and the obligation to buy the stock also at the ATM strike if the options are assigned.

By selling two options, you significantly increase the income you would have achieved from selling a put or a call alone. But that comes at a cost. You have unlimited risk on the upside and substantial downside risk.

THE MECHANICS
You simultaneously buy and sell the ATM call and the ATM put.

PROBABILITY OF SUCCESS
This type of trade has a probability of success of around 65%, but have a very small probability that you can collect 100% of the premium received, because you need the stock to finish right at your short strike at expiration.

TIPS
1. Do this trade only if you are anticipating minimal movement on the stock.
2. You might want to see the probability of ITM of the options that are trading away from the ATM strike added and subtracting your credit received. That way you can rapidly see your approximate probability of profit of the trade.
3. Try to place this type of trades 20 to 30 days to expiration.
4. This is also a good situational trade for a high volatility environment. You can collect a larger credit, thus giving you a higher range to profit from.

TRADE EXAMPLE
IBM is now trading at $97.00, so you decide to sell the $97.00 put and the $97.00 call for a net credit of $6.00.

MAXIMUM GAIN
Your maximum profit is realized when the stock settles at the ATM strike price at expiration. However, that's extremely difficult to predict.

In this example, if IBM closes at $97.00 at expiration, your spread will have its maximum worth, because both the call and the put will expire worthless.

EXITING THE TRADE

If you placed a straddle as a situational trade to take advantage of a reduction in implied volatility due to some news or earnings announcement, be ready to take the trade off after your catalyst has occurred.

MAXIMUM LOSS

A short straddle has a theoretically unlimited risk both to the upside and to the downside. If the stock goes up, your losses could be theoretically unlimited. If the stock goes down, your losses may be substantial, but limited to the strike price minus net credit received for selling the straddle. Thankfully, stocks can only go to Zero.

BREAK EVEN

On a short straddle, there are two break-even points:
- The ATM Strike minus the net credit received
- The ATM Strike plus the net credit received.

In our IBM example, our break evens will be $97.00 + $6.00 = $103.00 and $97.00 - $6.00 = $91.00.

CAPITAL REQUIRED OR BUYING POWER REDUCTION

This type of trade can only be performed in a margin account or portfolio margin account. You will also need naked option selling approval from your broker. The margin required for a short straddle is the short put or the short call regular margin required (whichever one is greater), plus the premium received from the other side.

VOLATILITY

This is a Vega negative, so after the play is established, you want implied volatility to reduce.

- If Volatility Increases: Negative Effect
- If Volatility Decreases: Positive Effect

After a play is established, you really want implied volatility to decrease. An increase in implied volatility is dangerous, because it works doubly against you by increasing the price of both options you sold. That means if you wish to close your position prior to expiration, it will be more expensive to buy back those options.

An increase in implied volatility also suggests an increased possibility of a price swing, whereas you want the stock price to remain stable around the ATM strike.

THETA

Passage of Time: Positive

For this type of trade, the net effect of time decay is positive and is also your best friend. It works doubly in your favor, eroding the price of both options you sold. That means if you choose to close your position prior to expiration, it will be less expensive to buy it back.

ADJUSTMENT

The only adjustment you can do is to move your untested side up or down (calls or puts) to or close to the new ATM strike, in order to collect additional credit. In this adjustment you will be considered to be upside down on your trade, because the calls and puts are on the wrong side the price action.

TRADE SUMMARY

Name:	Short Straddle
Assumption:	Neutral Strategy
Type:	Credit Spread
Max Profit:	Credit Received
Max Loss:	Theoretically unlimited to both sides.
Tips:	Do this trade to take advantage of High Implied Volatility.
	Then take the trade off after the catalyst has occurred

Break Even:	The ATM Strike minus the net credit received
	and the ATM Strike plus the net credit received.

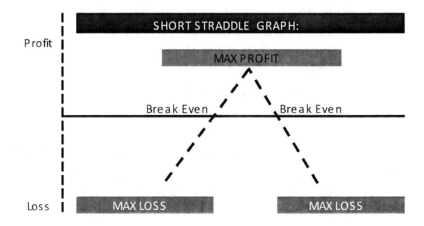

STRATEGY # 20

SHORT STRANGLE

This one of Tom and Tony's favorite plays, because it has a high probability of success. This type of trade can be used to raise overall portfolio probability of success, and should be a part of every high probability investing plan.

DEFINITION

A short strangle is the simultaneous sale of an OTM call and an OTM Put.

A short strangle is like an iron condor, without buying the outside wings. A long strangle, on the other hand, is exactly the opposite - it is buying an OTM call and OTM put. Tom and Tony never buy long strangles, because they have a very small probability of success and they are theta negative.

In order to make money on a long strangle you need a very large move. So for this reason we can forget about the long strangle and focus on one of the best trading strategies the short strangle.

DIRECTIONAL ASSUMPTION

A short strangle trade is considered a neutral strategy; you're expecting minimal movement on the stock.

A short strangle gives you the obligation to sell the stock at the OTM call strike sold, and the obligation to buy the stock also at the OTM put strike if the options are assigned.

By selling two options, you significantly increase the income you would have achieved from selling a put or a call alone. But that comes at a cost. You have unlimited risk on the upside and substantial downside risk.

THE MECHANICS
You simultaneously sell the OTM call and the OTM put.

PROBABILITY OF SUCCESS
Depending on what strikes you choose for this trade, the probability of success will vary. If you choose the 1 STD strikes, you will have around 68% probability of profit and if you go 2 STD, you will have around 95% probability of success.

TIPS
1. The further OTM the strike prices are, the lower the net credit received, but the higher the probability of success for the trade.
2. Try to place this type of trade 20 to 50 days to expiration.
3. This is also a good situational trade for a high volatility environment. You can collect a larger credit, thus giving you a higher range to profit from.

TRADE EXAMPLE
IBM is now trading at $100.00, so you decide to sell the $85.00 put and the $115.00 call for a net credit of $2.00.

MAXIMUM GAIN
Potential profit is limited to the net credit received.

This will happen if IBM closes between $85.00 and $115.00 at expiration, when your spread will have maximum worth, because both the call and the put will expire worthless.

MAXIMUM LOSS

A short strangle has theoretically unlimited risk both to the upside and to the downside. If the stock goes up past your short call strikes, your losses could be theoretically unlimited. If the stock goes down, your losses may be substantial, but limited to the strike price minus net credit received for selling the strangle. Thankfully stocks can only go to Zero.

BREAK EVEN

On a short strangle, there are two break-even points:
- the OTM put strike minus the net credit received
- the OTM call Strike plus the net credit received.

In our IBM example, our break evens will be $85.00 - $2.00 = $83.00 and $115.00 + $2.00 = $117.00.

CAPITAL REQUIRED OR BUYING POWER REDUCTION

This type of trade can only be performed in a margin account or portfolio margin account; you will also need naked option selling approval from your broker. The margin required for a short strangle is the short put or the short call regular margin required (whichever one is greater), plus the premium received from the other side.

VOLATILITY

This is a Vega negative, so after the play is established, you want implied volatility to reduce.

- If Volatility Increases: Negative Effect
- If Volatility Decreases: Positive Effect

After a play is established, you really want implied volatility to decrease. An increase in implied volatility is dangerous, because it works doubly against you by increasing the price of both options you sold. That means if you wish to close your position prior to expiration, it will be more expensive to buy back those options.

An increase in implied volatility also suggests an increased possibility of a price swing, whereas you want the stock price to remain stable between the OTM strikes.

THETA
Passage of Time: Positive

For this type of trade, the net effect of time decay is positive and is also your best friend. It works doubly in your favor, eroding the price of both options you sold. That means if you choose to close your position prior to expiration, it will be less expensive to buy it back

ADJUSTMENTS
There are some adjustments you can make in case the trade goes against you.

- Move the untested (profitable) side either calls or puts to a strike that can help you collect some extra premium. Tom and Tony like to move the option to the 20 delta. The more aggressive the adjustment you make (30 to 50 delta), the more chance that it may reverse and hurt you.
- You can also move up the "tested" side to the 40 or 20 deltas. This adjustments costs money. Tom and Tony never move the tested side.
- You can roll the tested option to the next month, in order to give you more duration. I do this all the time.
- You can also sell ½ of your position to reduce risk.
- You can calendarize your tested side by buying one call or put for every 3 short options that you have on. The long dated option will expand, offering you some protection.

TIPS

1. Tom likes to sell strangles after a big move that inflates the risk premium or implied volatility. Also, sometimes sideways action in the stock comes after such an event.
2. Never do naked strangles on the VIX, because volatility can explode and hurt you.
3. Also never do naked strangles on stock that may be takeover candidates.
4. You cannot sell short strangles in an IRA.

TRADE SUMMARY

Name:	Short Strangle
Assumption:	Neutral Strategy
Type:	Credit Spread
Max Profit:	Credit Received
Max Loss:	Theoretically unlimited to both sides.
Tips:	Sell at 1 STD or 90% Prob of Expiring
	Collect at least 1 to 1.5% of underlying price.
	Sell 20 to 40 Days out
Break Even:	The ATM Strike minus the net credit received
	and the ATM Strike plus the net credit received.

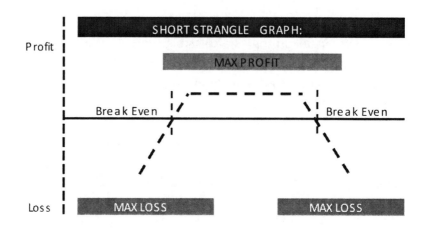

STRATEGY # 21
SYNTHETIC LONG STOCK
(aka LONG COMBINATION)

DEFINITION

When doing a long synthetic stock, buying the call gives you the right to buy the stock at strike price "X". Selling the put obligates you to buy the stock at strike price "X" if the option is assigned.

This strategy is often referred to as "synthetic long stock" because the risk/reward profile is nearly identical to long stock. Furthermore, if you remain in this position until expiration, you will probably wind up buying the stock at strike "X" one way or the other. If the stock is above strike "X" at expiration, it would make sense to exercise the call and buy the stock. If the stock is below strike "X" at expiration, you'll most likely be assigned on the put and be required to buy the stock.

WHY USE THIS STRATEGY?

Since you'll have the same risk/reward profile as long stock at expiration, you might be wondering, "Why would I want to run a combination instead of buying the stock?" The answer is **leverage**. You can achieve the same end without the up-front cost to buy the stock.

At initiation of the play, you will have some additional margin requirements in your account because of the short put, and you can also expect to pay a net debit to establish your position. But those costs will be fairly small relative to the price of the stock.

Most people who run a combination don't intend to remain in the position until expiration, so they won't wind up buying the stock. They're simply doing it for the leverage.

DIRECTIONAL ASSUMPTION
It is 100% bullish, since it is almost the same as purchasing stock outright.

THE MECHANICS
1. This strategy is normally done at the ATM strike, and it is normally done for a small credit.
2. You buy an ATM call and sell the ATM put on the same calendar month.

PROBABILITY OF SUCCESS
Since it is the same as having long stock, the probability of success is about 50%.

It's important to note that the stock price will rarely be precisely at strike price "X" when you establish this trade. If the stock price is above strike "X", the long call will usually cost more than the short put. So the play will be established for a net debit. If the stock price is below strike "X", you will usually receive more for the short put than you pay for the long call. So the play will be established for a net credit.

TIP
Remember: The net debit paid or net credit received to establish this play will be affected by where the stock price is relative to the strike price.

TRADE EXAMPLE
IBM is now trading at $100.00, so you decide to sell the $100.00 put and buy the $100.00 call for a net credit of $0.30.

MAXIMUM GAIN

There is a theoretically unlimited profit potential if the stock price keeps rising.

MAXIMUM LOSS

Potential loss is substantial, but limited to strike price "X" plus the net debit paid or minus net credit received. Remember, stocks can only go to zero.

BREAK EVEN

Strike "X" plus the net debit paid or minus the net credit received to establish the play.

In our IBM example, our break even will be $99.70, because we place the trade for a net credit.

CAPITAL REQUIRED OR BUYING POWER REDUCTION

The margin required for long combination is the same as the short put requirement.

VOLATILITY

After the trade is established, increasing implied volatility is somewhat neutral. It will increase the value of the option you sold (bad), but it will also increase the value of the option you bought (good).

THETA

For this strategy, time decay is somewhat neutral. It will erode the value of the option you bought (bad), but it will also erode the value of the option you sold (good).

ADJUSTMENTS

There is one cool adjustment you can make. If you are directionally correct in your assumption, you can potentially buy back the short put that you sold and keep the long call practically for free, or a small debit.

When you buy back your short put, you are also significantly reducing your margin, eliminating much of the trade's risk.

Another cool thing you can do is sell an OTM call against your synthetic stock, making it a kind of leveraged covered call, using much less capital than you would have invested in doing a simple covered call.

TRADE SUMMARY

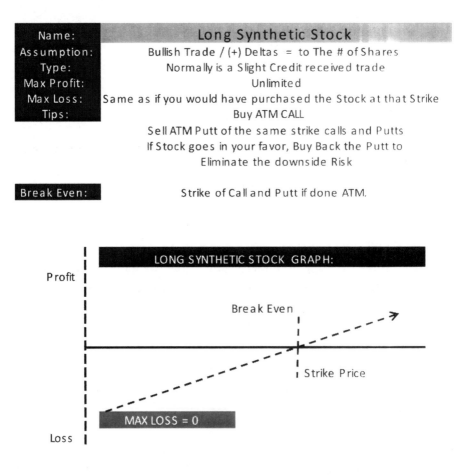

Name:	Long Synthetic Stock
Assumption:	Bullish Trade / (+) Deltas = to The # of Shares
Type:	Normally is a Slight Credit received trade
Max Profit:	Unlimited
Max Loss:	Same as if you would have purchased the Stock at that Strike
Tips:	Buy ATM CALL
	Sell ATM Putt of the same strike calls and Putts
	If Stock goes in your favor, Buy Back the Putt to Eliminate the downside Risk
Break Even:	Strike of Call and Putt if done ATM.

LONG SYNTHETIC STOCK GRAPH:

Profit

Break Even

Strike Price

MAX LOSS = 0

Loss

STRATEGY # 22
SYNTHETIC SHORT STOCK
(aka SHORT COMBINATION)

DEFINITION

When doing a short synthetic stock, buying the put gives you the right to sell the stock at strike price "X". Selling the call obligates you to sell the stock at strike price "X" if the option is assigned.

This strategy is often referred to as "synthetic short stock", because the risk/reward profile is nearly identical to short stock.

If you remain in this position until expiration, you are probably going to wind up selling the stock one way or the other. If the stock price is above strike "X" the call will be assigned, resulting in a short sale of the stock. If the stock price is below strike "X", it would make sense to exercise your put and sell the stock. However, most investors who run this strategy don't plan to stay in their position until expiration.

WHY USE THIS STRATEGY?

Since you'll have the same risk/reward profile as short stock at expiration, you might be wondering, "Why would I want to run a combination instead of selling the stock?" The answer is leverage. You can achieve the same end without the up-front cost of shorting the stock.

When you first put the trade on, you will most likely receive a net credit, but you will have some additional margin requirements in your account because of the short call. However, those costs will be fairly small relative to the margin requirement for short stock. That's the reason some investors run this play: to avoid having too much cash tied up in margin created by a short stock position.

Most people who run a combination don't intend to remain in the position until expiration, so they won't wind up selling or shorting the stock. They're simply doing it for the leverage.

DIRECTIONAL ASSUMPTION
It is 100% bearish, since it is almost the same as purchasing stock outright.

THE MECHANICS
1. This strategy is normally done at the ATM Strike. Also it is normally done for a small credit.
2. You buy an ATM put and sell the ATM call on the same calendar month.

PROBABILITY OF SUCCESS
Since it is the same as having short stock, the probability of success is about 50%.

It's important to note that the stock price will rarely be precisely or strike price"X" when you establish this strategy. If the stock price is above strike "X", you'll receive more for the short call than you pay for the long put. So the play will be established for a net credit. If the stock price is below strike "X", you will usually be established for a net debit.

TIP
Remember: The net credit received or net debit paid to establish this play will be affected by where the stock price is, relative to the strike price.

TRADE EXAMPLE

IBM is now trading at $100.00 so you decide to sell the $100.00 call and buy the $100.00 put for a net credit of $0.30.

MAXIMUM GAIN

The potential profit is substantial if stock goes to zero, but limited to strike price "X" plus the net credit received or minus the net debit paid to establish the trade.

MAXIMUM LOSS

Risk is theoretically unlimited if the stock price keeps rising.

BREAK EVEN

Strike "X" plus the net debit paid or minus the net credit received to establish the play.

In our example, our IBM breakeven will be $100.30, because we place the trade for a net credit.

CAPITAL REQUIRED OR BUYING POWER REDUCTION

The margin required for short combination is the same as the short call requirement.

VOLATILITY

After the trade is established, increasing implied volatility is somewhat neutral. It will increase the value of the option you sold (bad), but it will also increase the value of the option you bought (good).

THETA

For this strategy, time decay is somewhat neutral. It will erode the value of the option you bought (bad), but it will also erode the value of the option you sold (good).

ADJUSTMENTS

There is one cool adjustment you can make. If you are directionally correct in your assumption, you can potentially buy back the short call that you sold and keep the long put practically for free, or for a small debit.

When you buy back your short call, you are also significantly reducing your margin eliminating much of the trade's risk.

Another cool thing you can do is sell an OTM put against your synthetic stock, making it a kind of leveraged covered put, using much less capital than you would have invested in doing a simple covered put.

TRADE SUMMARY

Name:	Short Synthetic Stock
Assumption:	Bearish Trade / (-) Deltas = to The # of Shares
Type:	Normally is a Slight Credit received trade
Max Profit:	Unlimited up to ZERO
Max Loss:	Same as if you would have sold short the Stock at that Strike
Tips:	Buy ATM Put
	Sell ATM Call of the same strike calls and Putts
	If Stock goes in your favor, Buy Back the Call to
	Eliminate the upside Risk
	Strike of Call and Putt if done ATM.
Break Even:	Strike of Call and Putt if done ATM.

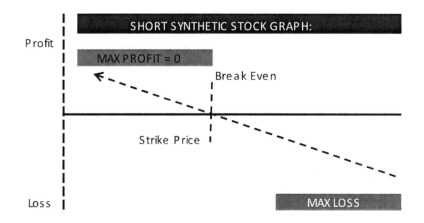

STRATEGY # 23
UNBALANCED IRON CONDOR

DEFINITION
Similar to a traditional iron condor, an unbalanced iron condor is a combination of two short vertical spreads (calls and puts). However, in this type of iron condor, one leg or wing has wider strikes than the other side. This allows the potential elimination of risk on one side or the other, while providing the advantages of an iron condor with directional bias.

Another way to create the "imbalance" is by selling a larger number of verticals on one side than the other.

DIRECTIONAL ASSUMPTION
Unbalancing a standard iron condor adds more risk to one of the sides of the trade. Having a directional bias is very important when putting on this strategy.

EXAMPLES
Let´s first look at a regular iron condor.

IBM is trading at $95.00 now.

Sell one call to open of IBM Sept 99

Buy one call to open of IBM Sept 100
** (One wide on each side, and 4 strikes between both our short options)
Sell one put to open of IBM Sept 91
Buy one put to open of IBM Sept 90

This type of Iron Condor is considered to be neutral, because both the width of the strikes and the distance between the short strikes are the same.

Constructing a Bullish Unbalanced iron condor
If you are bullish on IBM trading $95 now you want to unbalance the iron condor to the upside.

OPTION # 1, Unbalance the iron condor by widening the strikes of the put side
Sell one call to open of IBM Sept 99
Buy one call to open of IBM Sept 100
** (One wide on the call side, and two wide on the put side)
Sell one put to open of IBM Sept 92
Buy one put to open of IBM Sept 90

Here, as we can see, the put vertical is two wide compared to the call side which is one wide. This creates more credit and also more risk to the downside. We do this if we are bullish.

OPTION # 2, Unbalance the iron condor by selling more contracts on the put side.
Sell one call to open of IBM Sept 99
Buy one call to open of IBM Sept 100
** (We did double the number of contracts on the puts side, with both sides 1 wide)
Sell two puts to open of IBM Sept 91
Buy two puts to open of IBM Sept 90

In this example, we left the width of the strikes the same but doubled the number of contracts on the put side, making this trade a bullish trade.

Constructing a Bearish Unbalanced iron condor:
If you are bearish on IBM trading at $95 now, you want to unbalance the iron condor to the downside.

OPTION # 1, Unbalance the iron condor by widening the strikes of the call side
Sell one call to open of IBM Sept 98
Buy one call to open of IBM Sept 100
** (One wide on the put side, and two wide on the call side)
Sell one put to open of IBM Sept 91
Buy one put to open of IBM Sept 90

Here, as we can see, the call vertical is two wide compared to the put side which is one wide. This creates more credit and more risk to the upside. We do this if we are bearish.

OPTION # 2, Unbalance the iron condor by selling more contracts on the call side
Sell two calls to open of IBM Sept 99
Buy two calls to open of IBM Sept 100
** (We did double the number of contracts on the call side, with both sides 1 wide)
Sell one put to open of IBM Sept 91
Buy one put to open of IBM Sept 90

In this example we left the width of the strikes the same, but doubled the number of contracts on the call side, making this trade a bearish trade.

MAXIMUM GAIN

There are two scenarios where it is possible to make money on an unbalanced iron condor. Both depend on where the underlying stock is trading.

Scenario # 1: If the underlying stock trades between the short strikes at expiration, you collect your full credit thus creating your maximum gain.

Scenario # 2: The stock can move against you towards your non-skewed side (the side with the regular strike width or the side with the regular number of contracts), and still break even or collect a small profit. If the stock goes against your assumption, meaning you were wrong directionally, then the loss on the trade will be larger than on a regular iron condor.

MAXIMUM LOSS

Since we have two ways of unbalancing iron condor, we have two different ways to calculate maximum loss.

If you unbalanced the condor by widening one side, your max loss will be the width of the wider strikes minus the credit received.

If you unbalanced the condor by the number of contracts, the risk increases substantially. Your risk equals the width between the strike prices, times the number of contracts traded, minus the credit received.

CAPITAL REQUIRED OR BUYING POWER REDUCTION

The buying power necessary to trade an iron condor is equal to the maximum loss on the entire position. The requirement is not the risk of both the short call vertical and the short put vertical, because only one can lose at expiration.

GREEKS OF AN UNBALANCED IRON CONDOR

- Delta, positive if unbalanced with a bullish bias, negative deltas if unbalanced with a bearish bias.
- Gamma, Negative.

- Theta, Positive.
- Vega, Negative.

TRADE SUMMARY

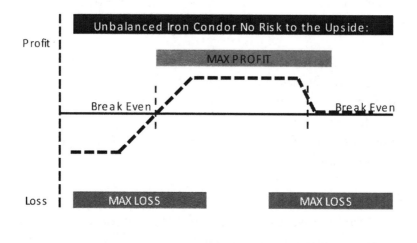

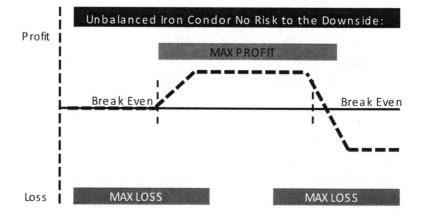

STRATEGY # 24
SKEWED IRON CONDOR

DEFINITION

A skewed iron condor is simply a regular iron condor that is skewed either bullish or bearish, depending on the selection of your short strikes.

This type of iron condor has the same number of contracts on either side and also has the same width of the strikes on both wings.

EXAMPLES

Let´s first look at a regular iron condor.

IBM is trading at $95.00 now.
Sell one call to open of IBM Sept 99
Buy one call to open of IBM Sept 100
*** (One wide on each side, and 4 strikes between both our short options)*
Sell one put to open of IBM Sept 91
Buy one put to open of IBM Sept 90

Here, as we can see, the call verticals have the same width, we did the same number of contracts on both sides, and the IC is situated pretty much in the middle of our sweet spot. This would be considered a neutral trade.

Skewing a regular iron condor Bullishly

If you are bullish on IBM trading $95 now, you want to skew the iron condor to the upside.

In this type of trade we don't change the number of contracts or the width of the strikes; we skew it by moving the location of our short strikes. If we are bullish, we will sell our put wing closer to the ATM strike and the call side further OTM.

Sell one call to open of IBM Sept 100
Buy one call to open of IBM Sept 101
** (The put side is closer to the current ATM price, than the call side.)
Sell one put to open of IBM Sept 94
Buy one put to open of IBM Sept 93

Skewing a regular iron condor Bearishly

If you are bearish on IBM trading $95 now, you want to unbalance the iron condor to the upside.

In this type of trade we don't change the number of contracts or the width of the strikes; we skew it by moving the location of our short strikes. If we are bearish, we will sell our call wing closer to the ATM strike and the put side further OTM.

Sell one call to open of IBM Sept 96
Buy one call to open of IBM Sept 97
** (The call side is closer to the current ATM price, than the call side.)
Sell one put to open of IBM Sept 91
Buy one put to open of IBM Sept 90

The main difference between a regular iron condor and a skewed iron condor is that you must be more directionally right on your assumption with a skewed iron condor, because you will have a much smaller margin of error, due to the fact that in order to skew the trade you had to place one of wings of the iron condor closer to the ATM strike.

TRADE SUMMARY

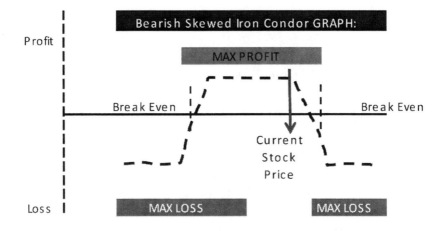

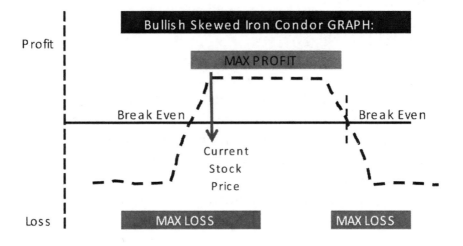

STRATEGY # 25
SKIP STRIKE BUTTERFLY WITH CALLS
(aka BROKEN WING BUTTERFLY WITH CALLS)

DEFINITION

A Call Broken Wing Butterfly Spread, also known as the Broken Wing Call Butterfly Spread or Skip Strike Butterfly Spread, is a variant of the butterfly spread options trading strategy. It is similar to the regular butterfly spread that is a neutral options strategy, but unlike the butterfly spread, it transfers all the risk of loss when the stock breaks downwards onto the upwards side. This means that the Call Broken Wing Butterfly Spread does not lose money when the stock goes downwards, but will lose more money than a butterfly spread if the stock rallies. This is particularly useful when the stock is expected to either stay stagnant or break downwards.

TIP

Butterfly spreads make most of their money near expiration day.

DIRECTIONAL ASSUMPTION

You are slightly bullish. You want the stock to rise to your short strike sold and then stop.

THE MECHANICS

1. A Call Broken Wing Butterfly Spread can be created simply by buying a further OTM call option instead of call options at the same distance from the middle strike price as the ITM call options.
2. You normally have to analyze four equidistant option strikes to put on this trade. You buy one OTM call at Strike 1, then you sell two of the Strike 2 calls. These strikes can be one , two or five wide, what is important is that you maintain the distance between strikes while doing the trade. Then you skip strike 3, and buy one call at strike 5.
3. Since this is low probability trade, the amount of capital you assign to this type of strategy should be much less than your regular lot or trade size.

Because butterflies widen much more on expiration week, you can put on this type of trade closer to expiration, thus having a bit more certainty about where the stock might end up at expiration.

TIPS

1. Tom and Tony like to do this type of trade for a small credit or for even. They normally do not like to pay a debit for this type of spread. They also use this strategy a lot for earnings announcements.
2. Due to the narrow sweet spot or profit area and the fact you're trading four different options in one play, skip strike butterflies may be better suited for more advanced option traders.

TRADE EXAMPLE

IBM is now trading at $97.00.

OTM Skipped Strike Call Butterfly Example: (Slightly bullish trade) – 2 strikes wide
Buy one $98 Call
Sell two $100 Calls
Skip over strike $102 and
Buy one $104 Call
for a net credit of $0.10 cents.

Essentially you're selling the short call spread to help pay for the butterfly.

In our IBM example, you are selling the $102/$104 two wide short call spread inside the regular butterfly.

Because establishing those spreads separately would entail both buying and selling a call with strike # 3, they cancel each other out, and it becomes a dead strike.

The embedded short call spread makes it possible to establish this trade for a net credit or a relatively small net debit. However, due to the addition of the short call spread, there is more risk than with a traditional butterfly.

A skip strike butterfly with calls is more of a directional play than a standard butterfly. Ideally, you want the stock price to increase somewhat, but not beyond your short strikes.

In our example, the calls with strikes $100 and $102 will approach zero, but you'll retain the premium for the call with strike $98.

This strategy is usually run with the stock price at or around ATM or slightly OTM. That helps manage the risk, because the stock will have to make a significant move upward before you encounter the maximum loss.

TIP

Tom & Tony like to think of this play as embedding a short call spread inside a long butterfly spread with calls.

This table summarizes the differences between a regular butterfly spread and the Broken Wing Butterfly Spread:

Regular Butterfly Spread	Broken Wing Butterfly Spread
Two long strikes at equidistance from middle strike	Out of the money strike is further from the middle strike
Debit Spread	Zero Cost or Credit Spread
Lower margin requirement	Higher margin requirement
Lower Maximum Loss/Profit	Higher Maximum Loss/Profit

MAXIMUM GAIN

Potential profit is limited to the short strike ($100) minus the first purchased strike $98, minus the net debit paid, or plus the net credit received.

For example, in the IBM Call Butterfly:
$100.00 - $98.00 = $2.000 plus the credit received of $0.10 = $2.10

EXITING THE TRADE

Tom and Tony like to exit butterfly spreads when they can sell for double what they paid.

MAXIMUM LOSS

Risk is limited to the difference between the skipped strike ($102) and furthest purchased strike ($104), minus the net credit received or plus the net debit paid.

In our IBM example the risk would be $2.00 (-) minus $0.10 0 $1.90

BREAK EVEN

If established for a net credit (as in our graph shown later) then the breakeven point is "THE SKIPPED STRIKE" plus the net credit received when establishing the play.

    If established for a net debit, then there are two break-even points:
- the lowest purchased strike *($98)* plus net debit paid, and
- the Skipped Strike *($102)* minus net debit paid.

CAPITAL REQUIRED OR BUYING POWER REDUCTION

For a skipped strike long butterfly spread, the buying power reduction is equal to the difference between the strike prices of the short call spread embedded into this strategy. Or more simply, equal to the maximum loss of the trade.

VOLATILITY

After the trade is established, the effect of implied volatility depends on where the stock is relative to your strike prices.

    If the stock is at or near our short strike, you want volatility to decrease. Your main concern is the two options you sold at ($102). A decrease in implied volatility will cause those near-the-money options to decrease in value, thereby increasing the overall value of the butterfly. In addition, you want the stock price to remain stable around your short strikes, and a decrease in implied volatility suggests that may be the case.

If the stock price is approaching or outside the wings, in general you want volatility to increase. An increase in volatility will increase the value of the option you own at the near-the-money strike, while having less effect on the short options.

TIP

Butterflies are at their cheapest when volatility is high, because it is much harder to predict the final price of a stock on expiration when implied volatility is high, due to rapid price movement on the underlying.

THETA

Passage of Time: Positive

For this type of trade, the net effect of time decay is positive. Ideally, you want your short options to expire worthless.

TRADE SUMMARY

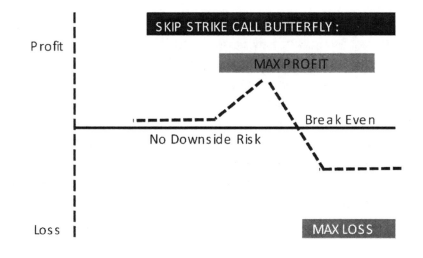

STRATEGY # 26
SKIP STRIKE BUTTERFLY WITH PUTS
aka BROKEN WING BUTTERFLY WITH PUTS

DEFINITION

A Put Broken Wing Butterfly Spread, also known as the Broken Wing Put Butterfly Spread or Skip Strike Butterfly Spread, is a variant of the butterfly spread options trading strategy. It is similar to the butterfly spread that is a neutral options strategy, but unlike the butterfly spread, it transfers all the risk of loss when the stock breaks upwards onto the downwards side. This means that the Put Broken Wing Butterfly Spread does not lose money when the stock rallies upwards, but will lose more money than a butterfly spread if the stock ditches. This is particularly useful when the stock is expected to either stay stagnant or rally.

TIP

Butterfly spreads make most of their money near expiration day.

DIRECTIONAL ASSUMPTION

You are slightly bearish. You want the stock to fall to your short strike sold and then stop.

THE MECHANICS

1. A Put Broken Wing Butterfly Spread can be created simply by buying a further OTM money put option, instead of put options at the same distance from the middle strike price as the ITM put options.
2. You normally have to analyze four equidistant option strikes to put on this trade. You buy one OTM put at Strike 1, then you sell two of the Strike 2 puts, (these strikes can be one, two or five wide, what is important is that you maintain the distance between strike while doing the trade). Then you skip strike 3, and buy one put at strike 5.

TIPS

1. Tom and Tony like to do this type of trade for a small credit or for even.
2. They normally do not like to pay a debit for this type of spread.
3. Also they use this strategy a lot for earnings announcements.
4. Due to the narrow sweet spot or profit area, and the fact you're trading four different options in one play, skip strike butterflies may be better suited for more advanced option traders.
5. Since this is low probability trade, the amount of capital you assign to this type of strategy should be much less than your regular lot or trade size.
6. Because butterflies widen much more on expiration week, you can put on this type of trade closer to expiration, thus having a bit more certainty as to where the stock could end up at expiration.
7. Tom and Tony like to think of this play as embedding a short put spread inside a long butterfly spread with puts.

TRADE EXAMPLE
IBM is now trading at $97.00.

OTM Skipped Strike Put Butterfly Example: (Slightly bearish trade) – 2 strikes wide

Buy one $96 Put
Sell two $94 Puts
Skip over strike $92 and
Buy 1 $90 Put for a net credit of $0.10 cents.

Essentially you're selling the short put spread to help pay for the butterfly.

In our IBM example, you are selling the $92/$90 two wide short put spread inside the regular butterfly.

Because establishing those spreads separately would entail both buying and selling a put with strike # 3, they cancel each other out and it becomes a dead strike.

The embedded short put spread makes it possible to establish this trade for a net credit or a relatively small net debit. However, due to the addition of the short put spread, there is more risk than with a traditional butterfly.

A skip strike butterfly with puts is more of a directional play than a standard butterfly. Ideally, you want the stock price to fall somewhat, but not beyond your short strikes.

In our example, the puts with strikes $94 and $92 will approach zero, but you'll retain the premium for the put with strike $96.

This strategy is usually run with the stock price at or around ATM or slightly OTM. That helps manage the risk, because the stock will have to make a significant move downward before you encounter the maximum loss.

This table summarizes the differences between a regular butterfly spread and the Broken Wing Butterfly Spread:

Regular Butterfly Spread	Broken Wing Butterfly Spread
Two long strikes at equidistance from middle strike	Out of the money strike is further from the middle strike
Debit Spread	Zero Cost or Credit Spread
Lower margin requirement	Higher margin requirement
Lower Maximum Loss/Profit	Higher Maximum Loss/Profit

MAXIMUM GAIN
Potential profit is limited to the highest strike put *($96)* minus the short strike *($94)* minus the net debit paid, or plus the net credit received.

For example in the IBM Put Butterfly:
$96.00 - $94.00 = $2.000 (+) plus the credit received of $0.10 = $2.10

EXITING THE TRADE
Tom and Tony like to exit a butterfly spread when they can sell it for double what they paid.

MAXIMUM LOSS
Risk is limited to the difference between the skipped strike ($92) and furthest purchased strike ($90) minus the net credit received or plus the net debit paid.

In our IBM examples the risk would be $2.00 (-) minus $0.10 or $1.90.

BREAK EVEN
If established for a net credit (as in the graph at the end of the strategy explanation), then the breakeven point is the skipped strike *($92),* minus the net credit received when establishing the play.

If established for a net debit, then there are two break-even points:
The highest strike put *($96)* minus net debit paid.
Or the skipped strike *($92)* plus net debit paid.

CAPITAL REQUIRED OR BUYING POWER REDUCTION
For a skipped strike long butterfly spread, the buying power reduction is equal to the difference between the strike prices of the short put spread embedded into this strategy. Or put simply, it's equal to the maximum loss of the trade.

VOLATILITY
After the trade is established, the effect of implied volatility depends on where the stock is relative to your strike prices.

If the stock is at or near your short strike, you want volatility to decrease. Your main concern is the two options you sold at $94. A decrease in implied volatility will cause those near-the-money options to decrease in value, thereby increasing the overall value of the butterfly. In addition, you want the stock price to remain stable around your short strikes, and a decrease in implied volatility suggests that way be the case.

If the stock price is approaching or outside the wings in general, you want volatility to increase. An increase in volatility will increase the value of the option you own at the near-the-money strike, while having less effect on the short options.

TIP

Butterflies are at their cheapest when volatility is high. The reason for this is that it is much harder to predict the final price of a stock on expiration when implied volatility is high, due to rapid price movement on the underlying.

THETA

Passage of Time: Positive

For this type of trade, the net effect of time decay is positive. Ideally, you want your short options to expire worthless.

TRADE SUMMARY

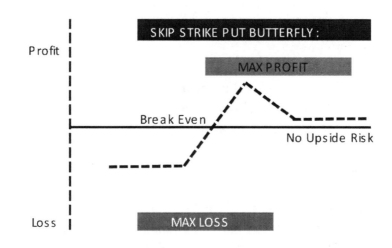

STRATEGY # 27
(OTM) DOUBLE DIAGONAL
aka CALENDARIZED IRON
CONDOR

DEFINITION
In this strategy, you're simultaneously running a short diagonal call spread and a short diagonal put spread. Both of those strategies are time-decay plays. You're taking advantage of the fact that the time value of the front-month option decays at a more accelerated rate than the back-month option.

DIRECTIONAL ASSUMPTION
In this strategy you want to capitalize on minimal stock movement over multiple option expiration cycles. Remember, you're anticipating minimal movement on the stock over at least two option expiration cycles.

THE MECHANICS
1. When you put this trade on normally, the stock will be trading halfway between both your front month strikes when you establish the strategy.
2. If the stock is not in the center at this point, the strategy will have a bullish or bearish bias.

3. You want the stock to remain between your short strikes, so the options you've sold will expire worthless, and you will capture the entire premium.
4. The longer dated OTM put and OTM call you bought both serve to reduce your risk over the course of the strategy, in case the stock makes a larger-than-expected move in either direction.
5. You should always try to establish this strategy for a net credit, but you may not be able to do so, because the front-month options you're selling have less time value than the back-month options you're buying.
6. It is possible to use back-month options with an expiration date that's further out in time. If you're going to use more than a one-month interval between the front-month and the back-month options, you need to understand the ins and outs of rolling an option position.

TRADE EXAMPLE
IBM is now trading at $100.00

Sell an out-of-the-money put, strike price $95 (Approx. 30 days from expiration — "front-month")
Buy an out-of-the-money put, strike price $93 (Approx. 60 days from expiration — "back-month")
And also
Sell an out-of-the-money call, strike price $105 (Approx. 30 days from expiration — "front-month")
Buy an out-of-the-money call, strike price $107 (Approx. 60 days from expiration — "back-month")
Generally, the stock price will be between our front month short strikes ($95 and $105)

MAXIMUM GAIN
Potential profit for this strategy is limited to the net credit received for the sale of the front-month options, *($95 & $105)* plus the net credit

received for the sale of the second round of options at the same strike prices, minus the net debit paid for the back-month options *($93 & $107)*.

Because you don't know exactly how much you'll receive from the sale of the additional options at strikes *($95 & $105)*, you can only "guesstimate" your potential profit when establishing this strategy.

MAXIMUM LOSS

The maximum loss is determined by taking whatever is greater, the dollar value of the difference between strikes of a short month call and back month call, or a short front month put and a long back month put, plus any debit paid, or less any credit received.

Maximum loss occurs if a stock settles either below the strike price of the long dated put, or higher than the strike price of the long dated call.

BREAK EVEN

It is possible to approximate your break-even points, but there are too many variables to give an exact formula, because you have at least one opportunity to roll front-month options to the back-month. However, you can estimate that your breakeven points will be between your short strike prices.

ROLLING OR EXITING THE TRADE

As expiration of the front-month option approaches, hopefully the stock will be somewhere between your short strikes. That is the best possible situation for this trade.

To complete this strategy you'll need to "roll" your short options, by buying to close the front-month options you originally sold, and selling another put and call of the same strikes - but now on the same expiration month as your back-month options. These options will have the same expiration as the ones you originally bought. This is known as "rolling" out in time.

Most traders buy to close the front-month options before they expire, because they don't want to carry the extra delta and gamma risk normally experienced on expiration week.

Once you've rolled your short options, and all the options have the same expiration date, you'll discover you've gotten yourself into a good old iron condor. The goal at this point is still the same as at the outset—you want the stock price to remain between your short strikes. Ultimately, you want all of the options to expire OTM and worthless, so you can pocket the total credit from running all segments of this strategy.

Some investors consider this to be a nice alternative to simply running a longer-term iron condor, because you can capture the premium for the short options on two consecutive expiration periods.

If one of the front-month options you've sold is ITM during the last week, it will increase in value much more rapidly than the back-month options you bought. So if it appears that a front-month option will expire ITM, you may wish to consider rolling your position before you reach the last week prior to expiration. That will reduce your delta risk.

CAPITAL REQUIRED OR BUYING POWER REDUCTION

For a double diagonal spread, the capital or margin requirement is the diagonal call spread requirement or the diagonal put spread requirement (whichever is greater). It is also the maximum loss of the entire position.

GREEKS

Delta, Neutral
    Gamma, Negative
    Theta, Positive,
    Vega, Positive

VOLATILITY

After the strategy is established, although you don't want the stock price to move much, it is desirable for the volatility to increase around the time the front-month options expire. That way, you will receive more premium for the sale of the additional options at your original short strikes.

After front-month expiration, the effect of implied volatility depends on where the stock is relative to your strike prices.

If the stock is near or between your short strikes, you want volatility to decrease. This will decrease the value of all of the options, and ideally, you'd like everything to expire worthless. In addition, you want the stock price to remain stable, and a decrease in implied volatility suggests that may be the case.

If the stock price is approaching or outside your back month strikes, in general you want volatility to increase. An increase in volatility will increase the value of the option you own at the near-the-money strike, while having less effect on the short options you sold.

TRADE SUMMARY

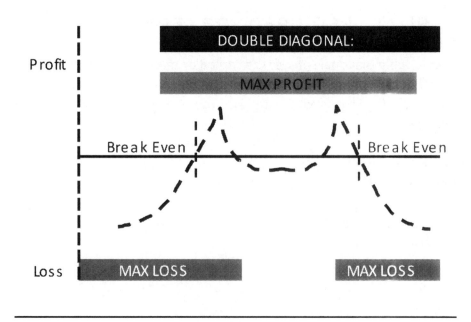

STRATEGY # 28
FRONT SPREAD WITH CALLS
aka RATIO VERTICAL CALL
SPREAD

DEFINITION
A Ratio Vertical spread is a combination purchasing a lower priced long call and sale of two higher priced calls, both options with the same expiration month.

DIRECTIONAL ASSUMPTION
It is a neutral to slightly bullish strategy. You want the stock to rise all the way to your short strike and stop, and not go past your short strike.

TIP
Due to the unlimited risk if the stock moves significantly higher, this strategy is suited only to the most advanced option traders. If you are not ready for this type of trade, consider running a skip strike butterfly with calls instead. That way you will be protected from a huge move to the upside.

THE MECHANICS

1. Buy a call with a 70% probability of expiring, and sell two calls with a 30% probability of expiring, or sell the 1st OTM call. **TIP:** You normally do the spread 1 or 2 strikes wide.
2. This strategy enables you to purchase a call that is ATM or slightly OTM without paying full price. The goal is to obtain the call with a lower strike for a credit or a very small debit, by selling the two calls with a higher strike price.
3. This strategy is like a Long Call Vertical spread on steroids, because one of the short calls will be uncovered.
4. If you do not want to have a naked position, consider buying the stock at the same time you set up this strategy. That way the second call won't be uncovered, and this strategy will be like a partially leveraged covered call.

TIP

Tom and Tony like to do this type of trade for a small credit or for even. They normally do not like to pay a debit for this type of spread. Also, they use this strategy a lot for earnings announcements.

TRADE EXAMPLE

IBM is now trading at $98.00 and you decide to buy one $97.00 call, and sell two $99.00 calls for a credit of $0.10 cents.

MAXIMUM GAIN

If established for a net debit, potential profit is limited to the difference between the lower strike and the higher strike, minus the net debit paid.

If established for a net credit, potential profit is limited to the difference between the lower strike and the higher strike, plus the net credit.

In our example, if IBM was at $99.00 at expiration, your two $99.00 short calls will expire worthless and the $$97.00 will be worth $2.00, *plus the $0.10 cents credit that you got when you place the trade, giving you a profit of $2.10*

MAXIMUM LOSS

If established for a net debit:
Risk is limited to the debit paid for the spread if the stock price goes down. Risk is unlimited if the stock price goes way, way up.

If established for a net credit:
Risk is unlimited if the stock price goes way, way up. Maximum loss is the difference between the long and short strike, minus the credit received or plus the debit paid.

BREAK EVEN AT EXPIRATION

If established for a net debit, there are two break-even points:
- The Lower Strike plus the net debit paid to establish the position.
- The Higher Strike plus the maximum profit potential.

If established for a net credit, there is only one break-even point, because you will not have any risk to the downside.

The breakeven will be the higher strike plus the maximum profit potential.

CAPITAL REQUIRED OR BUYING POWER REDUCTION

For this ratio spread, the capital requirement is the equal to the margin requirement of the naked short call.

VOLATILITY

This is a Vega negative trade, so after the play is established, you want implied volatility to rise.

If Volatility Increases: Negative Effect
If Volatility Decreases: Positive Effect

TIPS

1. After the trade is established, in general you want implied volatility to go down. That is because it will decrease the value of the two options you sold more than the single option you bought.

2. The closer the stock price is to the higher sold strike, the more you want implied volatility to decrease - for two reasons. Firstly, it will decrease the value of the OTM option you sold at the higher price more than the ITM option you bought at a lower strike. Secondly, it suggests a decreased probability of a wide price swing, and you want the stock price to remain stable at or around the higher strike and finish there at expiration.

THETA

Passage of Time: Positive

For this type of trade, the net effect of time decay is positive. For this play, time decay is your friend. It's eroding the value of the option you purchased (bad), however that will be outweighed by the decrease in value of the two options you sold (good).

ADJUSTMENT

At any time you can purchase a call higher than your short strike, in order to butterfly the tradeoff.

In our example where you are long one $97 call and short two $99 calls, (2 wide) you would then buy one of the $101 calls to butterfly off your position. Now your trade risk will be equal to the total debit paid for all three strikes.

Also, if the stock starts going down and your short calls start to lose their value, try to purchase the butterfly wing for the same amount that you received for your credit. That way you will have on a butterfly for free.

TRADE SUMMARY

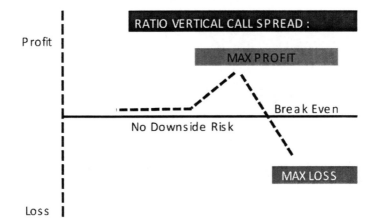

STRATEGY # 29
FRONT SPREAD WITH PUTS
aka RATIO VERTICAL PUT
SPREAD

DEFINITION
A Ratio Vertical spread is a combination of a purchase of a higher priced long put and selling two lower priced puts, both options with the same expiration month.

DIRECTIONAL ASSUMPTION
It is a neutral to slightly bearish strategy. You want the stock to fall all the way to your short strike and stop, and not past your short strike.

TIP
Due to the unlimited risk if the stock moves significantly lower, this strategy is suited only to the most advanced option traders. If you are not ready for this type of trade, consider running a skip strike butterfly with puts instead. That way, you will be protected from a huge move to the downside.

THE MECHANICS

1. Buy a put with a 70% probability of expiring, and sell two puts with a 30% probability of expiring or sell the 1st OTM put. **TIP:** You normally do the spread 1 or 2 strikes wide
2. This strategy enables you to purchase a put that is ATM or slightly OTM without paying full price. The goal is to obtain the put with a higher strike for a credit or a very small debit, by selling the two puts with a lower strike price.
3. This strategy is like a Long Put Vertical spread on steroids, because one of the short puts will be uncovered.
4. If you do not want to have a naked position, consider selling the stock at the same time you set up this strategy. That way, the second put won't be uncovered, and this strategy will be like a partially leveraged covered put.

TIP

Tom and Tony like to do this type of trade for a small credit or for even. They normally do not like to pay a debit for this type of spreads. Also, they use this strategy a lot for earnings announcements.

TRADE EXAMPLE

IBM is now trading at $98.00, and you decide to buy one $99.00 put, and sell two $97.00 puts, for a credit of $0.10 cents.

MAXIMUM GAIN

If established for a net debit, potential profit is limited to the difference between the two lower strikes, minus the net debit paid.

If established for a net credit, potential profit is limited to the difference between the two lower strikes, plus the net credit.

In our example, if IBM is at $97.00 at expiration, your two $97.00 short puts will expire worthless and the $$99.00 will be worth $2.00, plus the $0.10 cents credit that you got when you placed the trade, giving you a profit of $2.10.

MAXIMUM LOSS
If established for a net debit:
Risk is limited to the debit paid for the spread if the stock price goes up. Risk is unlimited if the stock price goes way, way down.

If established for a net credit:
Risk is unlimited if the stock price goes way, way down. Maximum loss is the difference between the long and short strike, minus the credit received or plus the debit paid.

BREAK EVEN AT EXPIRATION
If established for a net debit, there are two break-even points:
- The Higher Strike minus the net debit paid to establish the position.
- The Lower Strike minus the maximum profit potential.

If established for a net credit, there is only one break-even point, because you will not have any risk to the upside. The breakeven will be the lower strike minus the maximum profit potential.

CAPITAL REQUIRED OR BUYING POWER REDUCTION
For this ratio spread, the capital requirement is the equal to the margin requirement of the naked short put.

VOLATILITY
This is a Vega negative trade, so after the play is established, you want implied volatility to rise.

If Volatility Increases: Negative Effect
If Volatility Decreases: Positive Effect

TIPS

1. After the trade is established, in general you want implied volatility to go down. That is because it will decrease the value of the two options you sold more than the single option you bought.
2. The closer the stock price is to the lower sold strike, the more you want implied volatility to decrease for two reasons. Firstly, it will decrease the value of the OTM option you sold at the lower price more than the ITM option you bought at a higher strike. Secondly, it suggests a decreased probability of a wide price swing, whereas you want the stock price to remain stable at or around the lower strike and finish there at expiration.

THETA

Passage of Time: Positive

For this type of trade, the net effect of time decay is positive. For this play, time decay is your friend. It's eroding the value of the option you purchased (bad), however that will be outweighed by the decrease in value of the two options you sold (good).

ADJUSTMENT

At any time you can purchase a put lower than your short strike, in order to butterfly the tradeoff.

In our example you are long one $99 put and short two $97 puts (2 wide). You would then buy one of the $95 puts to butterfly off your position. Now your trade risk will be equal to the total debit paid for all three strikes.

Also, if the stock starts going up, and your short puts start to lose their value, try to purchase the butterfly wing for the same amount that you received for your credit. That way you will have on a butterfly for free.

TRADE SUMMARY

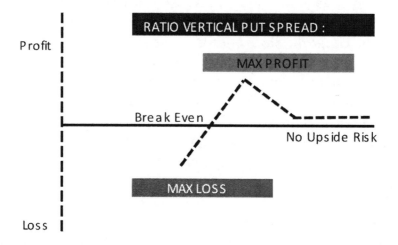

GOOD TRADE / BAD TRADE
CHEAT SHEET

On the following pages you will find a summary which I have prepared for you, showing you the right way and the wrong way of putting on trades.

When you can completely understand this trade summary, you will be ready to take the next step to more advanced trading concepts.

We have created a cheat sheet for each strategy - bullish, bearish and neutral.

Bullish Strategies

Stock: AAPL (Apple Inc) @$574.44 (A)

	The Trade (B)	Cost of trade / Credit (CR) or Debit (DBT) (C)	Probability of Profit (D)	Max Return on Capital Used (E)	Break Even Price of Underlying (F)	Difference of Current Stock price vs Strategy break even (A)-(F)	Good Trade or Bad Trade (GT/BT)
$574.44							
1	Buy Stock — Buy 100 shares of AAPL @$574.44	$57,444.00	50%	Unlimited	$574.44	$0.00	Neutral
2	Covered Call — B) 100 AAPL & S#1 July $590°C @ $15.30	$55,914.00	58%	2.74%	$559.14	$15.30	GT
3	Long Deep In The Money Call Naked — B) 11 July $560 Call $30.50	$3,050.00	37%	Unlimited	$604.94	$30.50	BT
4	Long Out of The Money Call Naked — B) 11 July $600 Call $11.70	$1,170.00	25%	Unlimited	$611.70	$37.26	BT
5	Long Call Vertical (ITM) B) One ITM & S) One OTM — B) July $565 C & S) July $575 C $5.48	$548.00	51%	82.48%	$570.48	$3.96	GT
6	Long Call Vertical (OTM) B) One OTM & S) One further OTM — B) July $580 C & S) July $590 C $4.40	$440.00	41%	127.27%	$584.40	$9.96	BT
7	Short Put Vertical (OTM) S) One OTM P & S) One further OTM P — S) July $550 P & B) July $540 P $2.80	$280.00	69%	38.89%	$537.20	$37.24	GT
8	Short Put Vertical (ITM) S) One ITM P & S) One further ITM P — S) July $590 P & B) July $580 P $5.77	$577.00	39%	136.41%	$584.23	$9.79	BT
9	Un-Balanced Iron Condor S) Puts 2 Wide & Sell Call 1 Wide — S) July $560/$550 P & S) $600/605 C $5.05	$505.00	67%	98.02%	$554.00	$20.44	GT
10	Short Put (Naked) Sell 1 OTM Putt — S) July $525 P (20 DELTA) $6.45	$635.00	80%	9.78%	$518.55	$55.89	GT
11	Upside Call Calendar (OTM) S) One Front MC & B) One Back Month C — S) July $595 C & B) AUG $595 C $9.83	$983.00	35%	28.09%	$556.00	$8.44	GT
12	Upside Putt Calendar (ITM) S) One Front MP & B) One Back Month P — S) July $595 P & B) AUG $595 P $10.53	$1,053.00	33%	29.00%	$570.00	$4.44	BT

Bearish Strategies
Stock: AAPL (Apple Inc) @574.44 (A) $574.44

	Stock: AAPL (Apple Inc) @574.44 (A)	The Trade	Cost of trade / Credit (CR) or Debit (DBT)	Probability of Profit	Max Return on Capital Used	Break Even price	Difference of Current Stock price vs Strategy break even	Good Trade or Bad Trade
	$574.44	(B)	(C)	(D)	(E)	(F)	(A)-(F)	
1	Sell Stock	Sell 100 shares of AAPL @574.44	$57,444.00	50%	Unlimited	$574.44	$0.00	Neutral
2	Covered Put	S) 100 AAPL & Sell 1 July $570 P @ $21.35	$55,309.00	66%	3.86%	$553.09	($21.35)	GT
3	Long Deep In The Money Put Naked	B) 11 July $585 Put $29.30	$2,930.00	39%	Unlimited	$603.74	$29.30	BT
4	Long Out of The Money Put Naked	B) 11 July $545 Put $11.95	$1,195.00	26%	Unlimited	$611.95	$37.51	BT
5	Long Put Vertical (ITM) B) One ITM & S) One OTM	B) July $585 P & S) July $575 P $5.40	$540.00	53%	85.19%	$570.40	$4.04	GT
6	Long Put Vertical (OTM) B) One OTM & S) One further OTM	B) July $550 P & S) July $540 P $3.00	$300.00	41%	233.33%	$583.00	$8.56	BT
7	Short Call Vertical (OTM) S) One OTM C & S) One further OTM C	S) July $550 C & B) July $540 C $2.80	$280.00	69%	38.89%	$537.20	($37.24)	GT
8	Short Call Vertical (ITM) S) One ITM C & S) One further ITM C	S) July $540 C & B) July $550 C $7.10	$710.00	35%	244.83%	$542.90	($31.54)	BT
9	Un Balanced Iron Condor S) Calls 2 Wide & Sell Puts 1 Wide	S) July 580/590 C & S) 540/545 P $5.62	$562.00	61%	77.94%	$554.00	($20.44)	GT
10	Short Call (Naked) Sell 1 OTM Call	S) July 615 C (20 DELTA) $7.35	$735.00	81%	6.53%	$517.65	($56.79)	GT
11	Downside Putt Calendar (OTM) S) One Front M P & B) One Back Month P	S) July $530 P & B) AUG $530 P $8.68	$868.00	33%	32.00%	$561.00	($13.44)	GT
12	Downside Call Calendar (ITM) S) One Front M C & B) One Back Month C	S) July $530 C & B) AUG $530 C $8.15	$815.00	35%	33.00%	$565.00	$9.44	BT

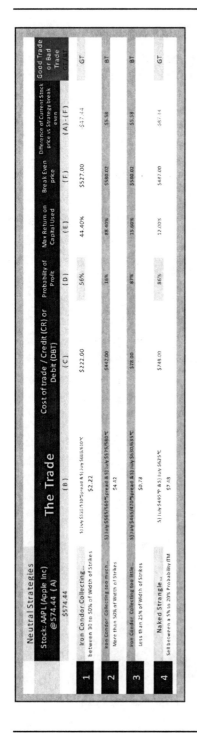

Neutral Strategies

Stock: AAPL (Apple Inc) @$574.44 (A) — $574.44

	The Trade (B)	Cost of trade / Credit (CR) or Debit (DBT) (C)	Probability of Profit (D)	Max Return on Capital Used (E)	Break Even price (F)	Difference of Current Stock price vs Strategy break even (A)-(F)	Good Trade or Bad Trade GT/BT
1	Iron Condor Collecting... Between 30 to 50% of Width of Strikes — S) July $520/530*Spread & S) July $615/610*C $2.22	$222.00	56%	44.40%	$527.00	$47.44	GT
2	Iron Condor Collecting too much... More than 50% of Width of Strikes — S) July $565/560*Spread & S) July $575/580*C $4.42	$442.00	16%	88.40%	$580.02	$5.58	BT
3	Iron Condor Collecting too little... Less than 25% of Width of Strikes — S) July $465/470*Spread & S) July $630/635*C $0.78	$78.00	87%	15.60%	$580.02	$5.58	BT
4	Naked Strangle... Sell between a 5% to 25% Probability ITM — S) July $495*P & S) July $625*C $7.48	$748.00	86%	12.00%	$487.00	$87.44	GT

CONCLUSION OF BOOK ONE

This concludes the basics of option trading strategies - Book One. In Book Two, we will learn some more advanced option strategies, as well as some of the most interesting and revealing trading insights that I was able to learn from Tom Sosnoff and Tony Battista.

Those insights are very important for you to learn, understand and apply if you wish to take your trading to the next level.

Before you learn more advanced strategies, we suggest you trade at least one to two thousand of the more basic trades.

Trade small, trade one lots if you need to, but put on as many fundamentally sound trades as you can, in order to "learn by doing". It is almost impossible to learn how to play golf by reading a book, and it's the same with trading - you need the repetition under several different environments. That experience will help you in your development as a trader.

Tom thinks you need to do at least 2 or 3 trades a day. That is equal to:

3 x 22 days = 66 trades a month
66 x 12 months = 792 trades a year.

I am currently doing about 10 to 12 trades a day, equal to about 2,500 to 3,000 trades a year.

I feel that for every 1,000 trades I do, I become a better trader, and it wasn't until after my first 10,000 trades that I really felt a big change in my trading results.

Furthermore, since you will be doing fundamentally sound trades that have more than a 50% probability of profit, you will have more winners than losers, and learning to manage your winners is the key to becoming the best trader that you can be.

Trade small,
Trade often,
Trade with a high probability of Success,
Manage your winners,
and
Good Luck Trading.

TRADER TERMINOLOGY & TRADING SLANG

When traders say **"we are getting short"** = It means that they are getting short the stock market in general.

When traders say **"I am short"** = It means that they are short the stock market in general.

When traders say **"I am Flat"** = It means that they are neutral, that they don't have a bias one way or the other, meaning they do not have much delta risk.

When traders say **"I am getting long"** = It means that they are buying the market in general.

When traders say **"I am Delta Long"** = It means that they have long deltas and would profit from an up move.

When traders say **"I am Delta neutral"** = It means that they do not have much Directional bias, and they would benefit from the market not moving by theta decay.

When traders say **"I want them to take juice out the market"** = It means that they want volatility to collapse, because they are short volatility.

When traders say **"I want the market to get pumped"** = It means that they want volatility to expand, and they want movement to the downside in order that volatility expands.

When traders say **"They are up 3 points"** = It means that the /Es E-Mini S&P futures are up 3 points, for every other instrument traders would specify the product before the move.

When traders say **"volume is really light"** = It means that volume in the overall market is light, and lower compared to the normally trading average.

When traders say **"this product stinks"** = It means that this product has not enough liquidity or volatility to make it interesting or viable for trading.

When traders say **"STOCK XYZ you cannot trade it"** = It means that this product has not enough liquidity or volatility, or does not have derivatives or does not have tight enough markets to trade it.

When traders say **"I am going to send it to the ICE"** = It means that you are sending your trade to the Inter-Continental Exchange, instead of sending it to BEST!

When traders say **"Pre-Market"** = It means about 2 hours before the market opens.

When traders say **"The Spot market "** = It is a cash market, and over the counter (OTC) market, like FOREX.

When traders say **"After Hours"** = The stock market closes at 4pm eastern but you can trade Index Futures products to 4:15pm and also a lot of very liquid stocks or ETF's like SPY.

Do traders use Stop Orders? = Traders normally do not use stop orders. Tom will very seldom use Stop Limit orders, and Tony will use stop market orders.

When traders say **"Buying Power Reduction"** = They are referring to the amount of money required in your account to do a trade.

When traders say **"Hard to Borrow"** = They are referring to stocks that are difficult to borrow by the brokerage house in order to get short.

Here are some **other examples of trading terminology** you must learn and understand if you want to belong "in the group".

To open a position is to establish a new position.

To open a long position is to establish a new bullish position.

To open a short position is to establish a new bearish position.

If you say **you going to short something**, it means you are bearish.

If you **say you are going long something**, it means you are bullish.

To "roll" a position is to take a position and move it from the front month to the back month.

Rolling up and out is when you move your short ITM calls or ITM spreads to a higher strike and to the following month.

Rolling Down and out is when you roll your short ITM puts or ITM spreads to a lower strike and to the following month.

A complex option strategy is one with more than one leg. The number of legs on a certain trade gives you the complexity of a trade.

When legging, you normally do not roll one leg, and leave the other leg on. Normally when you roll you roll all the legs.

To be legged out is where you tried to leg out your spread but you did not.

You can also **be "legged"** when you try to leg in into a position by establishing the 1st part of the trade 1st and then the 2nd part of the trade. If you cannot accomplish the second part, it is said that you are legged.

GLOSSARY OF TERMS

Assignment — Is the action when an option owner exercises the option, an option seller (or "writer") is assigned and must make good on his or her obligation. That means they are required to buy or sell the underlying stock at the strike price. The receipt of an exercise notice by an equity option seller (writer) that obligates them to sell (in the case of a short call) or buy (in the case of a short put) 100 shares of underlying stock at the strike price per share.

(ATM) At The Money — An equity call or put option is at the money when its strike price is the same as the current underlying stock price.

Back Month — For an option spread involving two expiration months, the month that is farther away in time.

(BEP) Break Even Point — An underlying stock price at which an option strategy will realize neither a profit nor a loss, generally at option expiration.

Call Option — An equity option that gives its buyer the right to buy 100 shares of the underlying stock at the strike price per share, at any time before it expires. The call seller (or writer), on the other hand, has the obligation to sell 100 shares at the strike price if called upon to do so.

Cash Settled Options — A settlement style that is generally characteristic of index or volatility options. Instead of stock changing hands after a call or put is exercised (physical settlement), cash changes hands. When an ITM contract is exercised, a cash equivalent of the option's intrinsic value is paid to the option holder by the option seller (writer) who is assigned.

Closing Trade — A transaction that eliminates (or reduces) an open option position. A closing sell transaction eliminates or reduces a long position. A closing buy transaction eliminates or reduces a short position.

Commission — The fee charged by a brokerage firm for its services in the execution of a stock or option order on a securities exchange.

Cost to Carry — The total costs involved with establishing and maintaining an option and/or stock position, such as interest paid on a margined long stock position or dividends owed for a short stock position.

Credit Trade/Spread — Any cash received in an account from the sale of an option or stock position. With a complex strategy involving multiple parts (legs), a net credit transaction is one in which the total cash amount received is greater than the total cash amount paid.

Debit Trade/Spread — Any cash paid out of an account for the purchase of an option or stock position. With a complex strategy involving multiple parts (legs), a net debit transaction is one in which the total cash amount paid is greater than the total cash amount received.

Delta — The amount a theoretical option's price will change for a corresponding one-unit (point) change in the price of the underlying security.

(ETF) Exchange Traded Fund — A security that represents shares of ownership in a fund or investment trust that holds a basket (collection) of specific component stocks. ETF shares are listed and traded on securities exchanges, just like stock.

EX Dividend Date — When a corporation declares a dividend, it will simultaneously declare a "record date" on which an investor must be recorded into the company's books as a shareholder to receive that dividend. Also included in the declaration is the "payable date", which comes after the record date and is the actual date dividend payments are made. Once these dates are established, the exchanges will then set the "ex-dividend" date ("ex-date") for two business days prior to the record date. If you buy stock before the ex-dividend date, you will be eligible to receive the upcoming dividend payment. If you buy stock on the ex-date or afterwards, you will not receive the dividend.

Exercise — To employ the rights an equity option contract conveys to its buyer to either buy (in the case of a call) or sell (in the case of a put) 100 shares of the underlying security at the strike price per share at any time before the contract expires.

Exercise price — A term of any equity option contract, it is the price per share at which shares of stock will change hands after an option is exercised or assigned. Also referred to as the "strike price" or simply the "strike."

Expiration day — The day on which an option contract literally expires and ceases to exist. For equity options, this is the Saturday following the third Friday of the expiration month. The last day on which expiring equity options trade and may be exercised is the business day prior to the expiration date, or generally the third Friday of the month.

Expiration Month — The calendar month during which a specific expiration date occurs.

Extrinsic Value — The portion of an option's premium (price) that exceeds its intrinsic value, if it is ITM. If the option is OTM, the extrinsic value is equal to the entire premium. Also known as "time value." (Theta)

Front Month — For an option spread involving two expiration months, the month that is nearer in time.

Gamma — The amount a theoretical option's delta will change for a corresponding one-unit (point) change in the price of the underlying security.

Historical Volatility — A measurement of the actual observed volatility of a specific stock over a given period of time in the past, such as a month, quarter or year. Tom likes to look at 30 days of historical volatility.

Implied Volatility — An estimate of an underlying stock's future volatility, as predicted or implied by an option's current market price. Implied volatility for any option can only be determined via an option pricing model.

Index Option--- An option contract whose underlying security is an index (like the SPX), not shares of any particular stock.

(ITM) In the Money — An equity call contract is ITM when its strike price is less than the current underlying stock price. An equity put contract is ITM when its strike price is greater than the current underlying stock price.

Intrinsic Value — The ITM portion (if any) of a call or put contract's current market price.

Leaps — LEAPS are long-term option contracts. Equity LEAPS calls and puts can have expirations up to three years into the future, and expire in January of their expiration years.

Long Option — A position resulting from the opening purchase of a call or put contract and held (owned).

Long Stock — Shares of stock that are purchased and held in a brokerage account, and which represent an equity interest in the company that issued the shares.

Margin Requirement — The amount of cash and/or securities an option writer is required to deposit and maintain in a brokerage account, to cover an uncovered (naked) short option position.

This cash can be seen as collateral pledged to the brokerage firm for the writer's obligation to buy (in the case of a put) or sell (in the case of a call) shares of underlying stock in case of assignment.

Opening Trade — A transaction that creates (or increases) an open option position. An opening buy transaction creates or increases a long position; an opening sell transaction creates or increases a short position (also known as writing).

Mean — For a data set, the mean is the sum of the observations divided by the number of observations. The mean is often quoted along with the standard deviation: the mean describes the central location of the data, and the standard deviation describes the range of possible occurrences.

Opening trade — A trade that creates (or increases) an open option position. An opening buy transaction creates or increases a long position; an opening sell transaction creates or increases a short position (also known as writing).

Options Pricing Model — A mathematical formula used to calculate an option's theoretical value using as input its strike price, the underlying stock's price, volatility and dividend amount, as well as time until expiration and risk-free interest rate. Generated by an option pricing model are the option Greeks: delta, gamma, theta, vega and rho. Well-known and widely used pricing models include the Black-Scholes, Cox-Ross-Rubinstein and Roll-Geske-Whaley.

(OTM) Out of the Money — A call option is OTM when its strike price is greater than the current underlying stock price. An equity put option is OTM when its strike price is less than the current underlying stock price.

Premium — The price paid or received for an option in the marketplace. Option premiums are quoted on a price-per-share basis, so the total premium amount paid by the buyer to the seller in any option transaction is equal to the quoted amount times 100 (underlying shares). Option premium consists of intrinsic value (if any) plus time value.

Put Option — An option that gives its buyer the right to sell 100 shares of the underlying stock at the strike price per share at any time before it expires. The put seller (or writer), on the other hand, has the obligation to buy 100 shares at the strike price if called upon to do so.

RHO — The amount a theoretical option's price will change for a corresponding one-unit (percentage-point) change in the interest rate used to price the option contract.

Roll — To simultaneously close one option position and open another with the same underlying stock, but a different strike price and/or expiration month. Rolling a long position involves selling those options and buying others. Rolling a short position involves buying the existing position and selling (writing) other options to create a new short position.

Short Option — A position resulting from making the opening sale (or writing) of a call or put contract, which is then maintained in a brokerage account.

Short Stock — A short position that is opened by selling shares in the market that are not currently owned (short sale), but instead borrowed from a broker/dealer. At a later date, shares must be purchased and returned to the lending broker/dealer to close the short position. If the shares can be purchased at a price lower than their initial sale, a profit will result. If the shares are purchased at a higher price, a loss will be incurred. Unlimited losses are possible when taking a short stock position.

Spread — A complex option position established by the purchase of one option and the sale of another option with the same underlying security. The two options may be of the same or different types (calls/ puts), and may have the same or different strike prices and/or expiration months. A spread order is executed as a package, with both parts (legs) traded simultaneously, at a net debit, net credit, or for even money.

Strike price — A term of any equity option contract, it is the price per share at which shares of stock will change hands after an option is exercised or assigned. Also referred to as the "exercise price," or simply the "strike."

THETA — The amount a theoretical option's price will change for a corresponding one-unit (day) change in the days to expiration of the option contract.

Time Decay — A regular phenomenon in which the time value portion of an option's price decays (decreases) with the passage of time. The rate of this decay increases as expiration gets closer, with the theoretical rate quantified by "theta," one of the Greeks.

Time value — For a call or put, it is the portion of the option's premium (price) that exceeds its intrinsic value (ITM amount), if it has any. By definition, the premium of ATM and OTM options consists only of time value. It is time value that is affected by time decay as well as changing volatility, interest rates and dividends.

Underlying Stock — The stock on which a specific equity option's value is based, which changes hands when the option is exercised or assigned.

VEGA — The amount a theoretical option's price will change for a corresponding one-unit (point) change in the implied volatility of the option contract.

Volatility — The fluctuation, up or down, in the price of a stock. It is measured mathematically as the annualized standard deviation of that stock's daily price changes.

Write — To sell a call or put option contract that has not already been purchased (owned). This is known as an opening sale transaction, and results in a short position in that option. The seller (writer) of an equity option is subject to assignment at any time before expiration, and takes on an obligation to sell (in the case of a short call) or buy (in the case of a short put) underlying stock if assignment does occur

INDEX

T

U

V

CPSIA information can be obtained at www.ICGtesting.com
Printed in the USA
LVOW11s1443160114

369729LV00016B/1210/P